The Well Balanced Child

Movement and early learning

Sally Goddard Blythe

Hawthorn Press

Published by Hawthorn Press, Hawthorn House, 1 Lansdown Lane, Stroud, Gloucestershire, GL5 1BJ, UK
Tel: (01453) 757040 Fax: (01453) 751138
info@hawthornpress.com
www.hawthornpress.com

2004000019

Cover photograph by Anna Marshall
Cover design by Hawthorn Press
Illustrations by Marije Rowling
Typesetting by Lynda Smith at Hawthorn Press, Stroud, Glos.
Printed in the UK by The Cromwell Press, Trowbridge, Wiltshire
Printed on acid-free paper from managed forests

British Library Cataloguing in Publication Data applied for

ISBN 1 903458 42 0

Contents

Foreword *by Harold N Levinson, MD.* ix
Guest Introduction *by Ewout Van-Manen* xii

Introduction 1
1. Genesis 4
   • Why Movement Matters to Your Child 4
   • Movement and Early Learning 6

2. Balance 10
   • Balance – the Primary Sense 11
   • Origins of Balance and Hearing 12
   • Development of Balance 14
   • Balance through Movement – Vital Training 16
   • A Sense of Direction 17
   • Balance and Learning 17
   • How is Balance Trained? 19

3. Brain and Body – Developing the Mind 21
   • Motor Development 24
   • Reflexes – Signposts of Development 24
   • Functions of Reflexes in Early Development. 27

4. From Cradle to Coordination:
   Reflexes and the Developing Mind 29
   • The Moro Reflex 29
   • The Tonic Labyrinthine Reflex (TLR) 33
   • The Asymmetrical Tonic Neck Reflex (ATNR) 40

- The Symmetrical Tonic Neck Reflex (STNR) 45
- The Rooting and Sucking Reflexes 51
- The Palmar and Plantar Reflexes 56
- Babinski Reflex 60
- The Spinal Galant Reflex 62

5. The Music of Language 66

6. Music and the Brain 77
- The Power of Singing 80
- Sound and Voice 82
- Music and the Brain 83
- What Else Does Music Do? 87
- Music and Number 88
- Arousal, Attention and Creativity 89

7. Of Many Minds 92
- What are the Implications of Different Stages
  of Brain Development for Education? 94
- Development, Learning Readiness, and Play 102

8. Feeding, Growth and the Brain .107
- Good Fats and Bad Fats 110
- Zinc 113
- Magnesium 117
- Calcium 118
- Manganese 121
- Social Context and Eating Patterns 123
- Biological Factors 124

9. Turning Children Around 130
- Space to Play 133
- Creating an Urban Utopia 135
- School Study 137

10. Learning from the Ancients: Education through
    Movement 164
- Oriental Education 165

- Greek Education 167
- The Roman Way 170
- The Age of Chivalry 172
- Kindergarten and Nursery School Provision 174
- Summary 175
- Conclusion 176
- General Themes in Child Development 177

Footnotes 179
General References 185
Resources 189

Appendix: Towards a Holistic Refoundation for Early Childhood: . . . .
The Hawthorn Press 'Early Years Series' 193

List of Figures

1.   Characteristics of the movement in the Womb – Piscean 7
2.   Movements characteristic of the first 4–6 months of life –
     Reptilian 7
3.   Movements in the Quadruped position – Mammalian 7
4.   From Crawling to Walking (hands still not entirely free
     from balance) – Primate 8
5.   Bipedal – Human 8
6.   The 3 Planes of Gravity/Axes for Operations in Space 15
7.   Hierarchical View of the Brain (The Evolutionary Brain) . . .26
8–9. The Moro Reflex 30
10. The Tonic Labyrinthine Reflex (TLR) Extension 34
11. The Tonic Labyrinthine Reflex (TLR) Flexion 34
12. Early attempts at Head Righting in the Prone Position 35
13–14. School Aged Child attempting to 'accommodate' the effect
     of a residual Tonic Labyrinthine Reflex (TLR) when sitting . .36
15–18. Infants in prone, sitting and standing positions showing line
     of gravity from head to toe 38
19. The Asymmetrical Tonic Neck Reflex (ATNR) 41
20. The Symmetrical Tonic Neck Reflex (STNR) in Flexion 45
21. The Symmetrical Tonic Neck Reflex (STNR) in Extension . .46

22–23. Sitting Positions Typical of an older child with a
        Symmetrical Tonic Neck Reflex (STNR) 47
24.   The Rooting Reflex 53
25.   The Sucking Reflex 53
26.   The Palmar Reflex 56
27.   The Plantar Reflex 57
28.   Infant Babinski Reflex 61
29.   The Spinal Galant Reflex 62
30.   The 3 Dimensions of Music 88
31.   The Tree of Knowledge: Stages of Maturation
        in the Central Nervous System 96

List of Tables

1.   Human Brain Waves and Associated States of Arousal 90
2.   Change in Neurological Scores and Percentile Rating Score
       on the Draw a Person Test before and after Nine months
       of Developmental Exercises in School 161

List of Abbreviations

ATNR – Asymmetrical Tonic Neck Reflex
DHA – Docosahexaenoic Acid
EFAs – essential fatty acids
Hz – herz
RAS – Reticular Activating System
STNR – Symmetrical Tonic Neck Reflex
TLR – Tonic Labyrinthine Reflex
VOR – Vestibular-Ocular-Reflex

Dedication

Over the last 15 years I have been particularly lucky to meet men and women who were world experts in their field. These were people of extraordinary intellectual and creative stature – pioneers who had spent a lifetime developing and testing their ideas.

Their published works often showed only a fraction of their thinking. In hearing them lecture and in discussing ideas with them, I have learned more than in a thousand pages of reading. With each one, I was struck by how these most brilliant of minds never belittled the ideas of others, and I have constantly been reminded that ideas are rarely born of individuals; rather, they are conceived as a result of thoughts and discussions shared. In other words, creativity is usually born from shared experience and the sparks that fly between.

This book is dedicated to all the men and women of ideas who have shared their thoughts and wisdom, and by so doing allowed the knowledge of today to be, and the dreams for tomorrow to exist.

Acknowledgements

My husband Peter, and my children James, Thomas, and Gabriella.

To Ewout Van-Manen, Professor Lyelle Palmer and Dr Harold Levinson for their time and generous contributions to this book.

To all the people who have been involved in the work of INPP over many years and in many different ways. All have contributed in some way to the work that INPP does today.

To Martin, Rachel and Richard at Hawthorn Press for all their help, advice and support and to Marije Rowling for her beautiful illustrations of babies.

Foreword

by Harold N Levinson, MD

The Well Balanced Child is a magnificently titled and highly informative book skilfully written by a dedicated therapist. This work explores the scientific essence underlying the age-old truth 'Sound body, sound mind', and explains why early movement is vital for developing *sound* balance as well as the interrelated and dependent foundations for normal or *sound* language, learning, cognition, and affect. In other words, according to the author the balance mechanism is rather like a piano that is genetically given to a child at birth. However, the child must learn to use and play the piano if the amazing potential and neuropsychological 'tunes' held within the immature brain are to unfold normally. And most important, the succeeding chapters provide all readers, especially interested parents, teachers, and other professionals, with the crucial new-age insights required to maximize sensory-motor and related cognitive functioning via balance enhancement in both normal and abnormal children.

In order to preserve focus and avoid needless confusion, this well-balanced content was sensibly designed to flow like a harmonious and soothing tune devoid of the harsh tones characterizing confusion and complexity. However, to properly understand this written melody's foreground in its true depth and scope, it appeared essential to highlight and emphasize its vital background. Thus, for example, upon recent independent validation, my three decade-old research effort has belatedly been credited with providing the first (1973) and most comprehensive understanding that the many and diverse symptoms characterizing dyslexia and related learning, sensory-motor, attention deficit, and anxiety or phobic disorders were caused by a medically diagnosable and treatable signal-scrambling dysfunction within the inner-ear and its 'super-computer', the cerebellum – the lower 'reflex' brain of man and the highest brain of most animals. Previously, these important insights, as well as those that follow here and contained within this important work, were scientifically overlooked or denied.

In addition, my research also demonstrated that dyslexia was not just a severe reading disorder characterized by reversals, as traditionally thought and defined. Rather, dyslexia was shown to be a cluster of many and diverse symptoms in varying intensities affecting such major areas of higher order functioning as reading, writing, spelling, mathematics, memory, speech, and so on. As a result, it became clear that a group of previously misunderstood and differently named higher order impairments affecting over 20 per cent of the population were merely symptomatic parts of the inner-ear/cerebellar-determined dyslexia syndrome. Most important, these symptomatic impairments of lower-brain origin responded favourably to inner-ear/cerebellar and interrelated cognitive enhancing therapies, and include: **Dyslexia** (poor reading), **Learning disabilities** (poor learning and memory), **Attention Deficit-Hyperactivity Disorder** (poor attention and activity levels), **Dyspraxia** (poor balance-coordination-rhythm), **Dysgraphia** (poor writing), **Dyscalculia** (poor mathematical skills), **Dysphasia** and **Dysnomia** (poor speech and word or name recall), **Asperger Syndrome** (poorly read social and feeling signals), **Anxiety Disorders** (sensory-motor and related phobias), **Mood and Self-Esteem Disorders** (poor mood and body-image functioning), and so on.

By contrast, for over a century the cognitive, emotional, linguistic, memory, concentration, and social functioning related to the above differently named inner-ear/cerebellar disorders were mistakenly believed to be due to diverse primary processing impairments within the higher thinking brain or cerebral cortex rather than to secondary difficulties in handling the distorted signals received from dysfunctioning lower brain 'fine tuners'. And so the therapeutic benefits derived from a series of non-medical inner-ear/cerebellar-enhancing therapies – such as sensory-motor integration, reflex inhibition, etc. – were also similarly denied, as was the prior crucial research of Jean Ayres, Peter Blythe – the author's mentor – and a host of other gifted clinicians and researchers.

In retrospect, the interdependent functional links between the lower and higher brains can be readily proven by a simple experiment. All the typical and even atypical symptoms characterizing dyslexia, attention deficit, anxiety and related balance-coordination-rhythmic disorders can be triggered in normal individuals following excessive spinning and dizziness. And all these many and diverse reading and non-reading symptoms can be significantly prevented or minimized by the prior implementation of inner-ear/cerebellar-enhancing medical and non-medical therapies similar to those used by the astronauts to prevent what I called 'space dyslexia' at zero gravity. Indeed, one can only marvel at the ingenious vestibular-based insights and predictions of the late neuropsychiatrist and psychoanalyst Paul Schilder: 'when we understand the balance mechanism we will understand the aetiology of neurosis' and that balance is essential for the most basic of functions in a gravity-based environment.

No doubt readers will wonder why the intuitively understood well-balanced body-mind title and related concepts and breakthroughs took decades before they found acceptance, especially since the dominant century-old thinking brain theories led absolutely nowhere scientifically in terms of comprehensive understanding, diagnosis, treatment, and even prevention of any of the previously mentioned disorders. Although I provided a fact-based psychoanalytic explanation for the scientific denial characterizing inner-ear/cerebellar disorders and research in *The Discovery of Cerebellar-Vestibular Syndromes and Therapies: A Solution to the Riddle – Dyslexia*, I believe Nobel Physicist Max Plank expressed it more simply and perhaps even better: 'Science progresses not by convincing the adherents of old theories that they are wrong but by allowing enough time to pass so that a new generation can arise unencumbered by the old errors.'

In summary, I believe the amazing depth and scope of the many and diverse balance and related sensory/motor and cognitive developmental insights presented within this intellectually captivating work are absolutely vital to all parents and professionals interested in children. Additionally, when this scientifically vibrant content is properly integrated with the patient-based cerebellar-vestibular medical insights contained within my recently updated work, *Smart But Feeling Dumb*, then a new and expanding therapeutic synergy is created. As a result, it is now possible for experienced clinicians to properly combine medical and non-medical inner-ear/cerebellar and interrelated cognitive enhancing therapies so that all suffering smart but dumb-feeling children and adults with signal-scrambling disorders can be significantly, rapidly, and often dramatically helped: Now all can feel as smart as they really are. And all can attain the dreams and ambitions that otherwise would never have been theirs.

Harold N Levinson, MD
Director, Levinson Medical Center for Learning Disabilities
www.dyslexiaonline.com

Guest Introduction

by Ewout Van-Manen

In time gone by, when people lived in more close-knit communities supported by neighbours, friends, and family, parenting was in some ways a much simpler task than it is in the twenty-first century. Well-off members of society employed professionals such as nannies to bring up and educate their children, and in the poorer families the whole community was involved, with the children spending much of their time helping their parents with many practical tasks.

Now, in the early part of the twenty-first century, parenting has become one of the hardest tasks to do well. On the one hand we have much less support from family and friends: mothers who have had successful careers often feel pressurized to return to work to maintain their place on the 'ladder', and many families depend on incomes from both parents to survive financially. We have a dearth of 'advice' from the media and government as to the way we should rear our children. Much of this information is confusing, with reports frequently being published or broadcast with conflicting views.

How do we sort through, and make sense of, this information in order to be in a position to make informed decisions as to what is best for our children? Clearly, the best way to begin to look at these issues is by looking at general child development. It is only by understanding child development and by observing the children in our care that we can begin to be in a position to make appropriate, informed judgements and decisions.

Psychologists and educationalists point to significant and sequential developmental stages in child development. At the beginning of the last century, the Austrian educationalist Rudolf Steiner described the first stage of child development (up to the age of the change of teeth at about age 7) as being primarily dependent on the child's physical organism. Some years later in the 1940s, the Swiss psychologist Jean Piaget observed that a child's physical movement is the basis for cognitive, social, and emotional development. If the physical sense of balance is not developed, there is likely to be a problem with mental equilibrium too. Problems in movement correspond to delayed language development; and if sensory development is impaired, the development of intelligence is interrupted and learning is hindered.

Unfortunately we live in a time when there is tremendous pressure for children to become literate early on in their lives. It is a time when children are being robbed of their childhood, when a significant amount of time is spent statically watching television, and when 'play' can mean sitting at a computer instead of being engaged in activities that stimulate and develop the senses of movement.

It is becoming more and more common for schools to have classes with many children who have not experienced appropriate amounts of sensory experience, movement, play, music, and speech. As a result, these children are not yet developmentally ready to make use of what education has to offer.

The development of motor skills, language acquisition, and visual and auditory competence must be taken seriously and intensely fostered. If these developments do not occur at the proper age, then although it is possible to compensate for this at a later stage, this can only be achieved with great effort and commitment.

Professor Dr Peter Struck, a German authority on child development,[†] reports that

'…children who have too seldom run and jumped, who have had insufficient opportunity to play on a swing or in the mud, to climb and to balance, will have difficulty walking backwards. They lag behind in arithmetic and appear to be clumsy and stiff. These children cannot accurately judge strength, speed, or distance; and thus they are more accident prone than other children.'

Of course, as parents we instinctively know that it is natural for children to be almost constantly engaged in movement. We cannot expect a small child to sit still for long periods as they are still learning to control their balance. Hopping, skipping, climbing, and balancing are all part of a child's learning to control their balance and body. Without the opportunity to move and progress through the early developmental stages, the brain is unable to develop the skills that are necessary for intellectual development. The (poor) Romanian orphan children who were kept in their cots and were deprived of movement, a chance to play and good nutrition experienced developmental delays as a result.

Professor Struck also reports that, in Germany:

'One in ten adolescents already suffers hearing loss; 60 per cent of the children entering school have poor posture, 35 per cent are overweight, 40 per cent have poor circulation, 38 per cent cannot adequately coordinate their arms and legs, and more than 50 per cent lack stamina for running, jumping, and swimming. The Hamburg Centre for Child Development alone annually treats 4,000 children who have movement and sensory disorders.'

A society that does not promote the sensory development of its younger generation is at the same time diminishing its overall intellectual capacity.

When I first came across the research and work of the Institute of Neuro-Physiological Psychology (INPP), I was fascinated. Here, there was research being conducted which looked at child development in a way which showed how the brain and movement interact in child development. I was struck by the fact that the work done by the INPP actually confirmed a common-sense approach to child rearing, and gave us a modern understanding of why movement, music, nutrition, etc. are vital to the development of the child.

The work of this book's author, Sally Goddard Blythe, as a researcher and NDD therapist has made a significant contribution to our understanding of child development and the neurological relationship between movement and learning. Both as a parent and as a Learning Support teacher, I have been greatly influenced and helped in my work with children by Peter Blythe's and Sally Goddard Blythe's research and insights. Although there are books and many papers available for education professionals and therapists, unfortunately there has not been much material suitable for the wider public – parents in particular. Until now, that is.

This book makes a major contribution towards sensible, informed parenting and educating. It provides the reader with a good introduction to the effect of retained primitive reflexes, music, and nutrition. In *The Well Balanced Child*, Mrs Goddard Blythe not only speaks out of her expertise as a neuro-physiological psychologist but also as an experienced mother.

Ewout Van-Manen
Waldorf Educator and parent, Michael Hall School

Note
† Peter Struck, *Yesterday's Education, Today's Pupils and Tomorrow's Schools*, Hanser Verlag, Munich, 1997.

Author's Note

This book is not intended to provide a prescription for how to bring up your child or how to educate a child (if such a thing were possible). Every child is different and every culture nurtures different strengths and values in its members. Within these individual differences there is a common theme, the theme of development – the universal factor shared by all children whatever their background and whatever their future.

In the following chapters, I have explored some of these universal factors and discussed their impact upon learning and emotional development. It is hoped that a deeper understanding of these themes or common denominators in development can help anyone involved in the care of children to provide the best possible environment in which our children can grow.

Sally Goddard Blythe
The Institute for Neuro-Physiological Psychology (INPP)
1, Stanley Street
Chester CH1 2LR

Tel. 01244 311414

Introduction

When my children were growing up, there was an abundance of literature in which the stages of child development were carefully chronicled and practical advice was provided on child care, but nowhere could I find an adequate explanation of *how* the dual processes of nature and nurture operate together to produce the skills that are uniquely human, such as language and creativity beyond the creativity of simple procreation.

When I started to work with children and adults who were experiencing problems, it soon became very clear that, irrespective of their presenting difficulties, all shared something in common. The demands of the environment outstripped the individual's ability to cope with the environment, and the more the child was coached, cajoled, bribed, or bullied into achieving, the greater the problem or emotional stress became.

The techniques of assessment and remediation developed at the Institute for Neuro-Physiological Psychology in Chester by Peter Blythe and his colleagues in the 1970s, now practised by students of the approach all over the world, provided a method of identifying definite developmental problems, revisiting the course of physical development and giving the brain a 'second chance' to make good the deficits that had occurred in early development and which continued to undermine the performance of the child at a later age.

In revisiting key stages of child development, I became fascinated by the functional impact of each stage of development. In other words, what does each stage of child development actually *do* in helping to build the architecture of the brain? Why does missing out one stage of development apparently affect later aspects of cognitive learning and emotional regulation in some people and not in others? This book is an attempt to answer some of those questions. It is not a book of new ideas; rather a new way of looking at long-accepted ideas and traditions that we are at risk of losing in our enthusiasm to embrace new inventions.

We live in an age where, increasingly, we distrust the evidence of our senses or our intuition. In Oriental medicine, the physician uses his senses to diagnose illness. Infection results in an alteration of body chemistry, which can be detected in the smell of the breath, colour and texture of the skin and hair, coating on the tongue, dullness in the eyes, and so on. Western medicine used to have to rely upon these same keen powers of observation, but increasingly the medicine man of the West must seek confirmation of his observations through complex laboratory tests and scanning equipment. We are approaching an age when, if we cannot measure it, it does not exist.

Whilst science – the testing of observations and ideas – constitutes an essential part of civilization and progress, intuition is the spark that lights the fire of scientific investigation. In looking at child development, I wanted to marry the processes of science and intuition, to find an explanation as to *why* certain social traditions and child-rearing practices have been consistently successful, despite a vastly changing world and a diversity of cultural ideals.

This book is an attempt to chart some of the processes of child development and environmental opportunity that remain constant themes through changing fads and fashions. It provides an introduction to the importance of movement for all aspects of life and living, paying particular attention to the physical role of *balance* – the first of the sensory systems to mature. The book tells a story of sensory-motor development through the early years, emphasizing the importance of movement, sensory experience, music, and environmental opportunity in priming the developing brain for later learning.

The process of motor development in the first year of life is described through a series of reflexes, which provide mirrors on the child's developing nervous system, whilst also providing an in-built training programme for motor skills. The development of language is viewed as a whole-body skill, with music in its broadest sense forming an intrinsic part of language. The role of nutrition, in helping to maintain sound body chemistry and also in facilitating social interaction and social development, is also discussed.

The effects of a movement programme in schools are illustrated through a mixture of case studies, individual stories, and children's letters and drawings. Finally, key aspects of the role of movement in education are traced from the ancient Orient through to the present day.

In an age of labour-saving devices and electronic toys for children and adults, when physical exercise is increasingly an additional 'task' rather than being a normal part of everyday living, the book is a reminder that physical experience is the very expression of life. Just as the brain controls the body, the body has much to teach the brain.

1. Genesis

'A child is on loan from God, entrusted to its parents. Its pure heart is a precious uncut jewel devoid of any form or carving, which will accept being cut into any shape, and will be disposed according to the guidance it receives from others.'

Al-Ghazali (1111)

Why Movement Matters to Your Child

From the very beginning of life there is movement. Just a few days after conception, inside a tiny ocean, an acrobat starts to perform. Beginning with gentle rocking movements in response to the inner ocean's tide, small primitive movements gather in strength until spontaneous movements and reflex responses gradually unfold. These early movements will eventually become part of the dance of development, the stages of which have been choreographed over the course of many millennia through the evolution of humankind.

These tiny movements are a human being's first outward expression of their experience of the world – the first language. They will also help to fashion the brain and are instrumental in the formation of millions of connections within the developing nervous system of the embryo, the foetus, and the growing child.

Repeated movements help to strengthen the neural pathways that run between the brain and the body. This network of connections will form the main system of communication between the individual and outside world.

The experience of movement is shared by every living thing, from the rotation of the earth on its axis to hearing the birds sing. Movement is present at the creation of human life, when unity of the sperm and egg takes place as a result of cellular movement. The subsequent process of cell division, protein structuring, and development can be seen as biological motility. Movement is also involved in each one of our sensory perceptions. Our experience of balance, for example, is actually a response to slow movement; hearing occurs when special receptors in the inner ear receive vibrations or sound waves travelling at speeds of between 125 and 16-20 000 hz. The eye detects the movement of photons of light travelling at faster speeds still. Photons come into contact with the retina, from where electrical impulses are sent to the brain, which then converts the signals into visual images.

Our language acknowledges that life and the experience of movement are inseparable. It used to be said that the baby had 'quickened' when the expectant mother felt her baby move for the first time; when something hurts, we say we are cut to the 'quick' or the point of feeling. When our emotions are strongly roused we feel deeply, and the modern word 'emotion' stems from the word *emovere* meaning 'to move'.

In this way, movement is an integral part of life from the moment of conception until death, and a child's experience of movement will play a pivotal part in shaping his personality, his feelings, and his achievements. Learning is not just about reading, writing, and maths. These are higher abilities that are built upon the integrity of the relationship between brain and body.

At birth, connections to higher centres in the brain are only tenuously made. This is rather like the neurological equivalent of preliminary sketches or a blueprint for a grand design. It will take many years for the blueprint to be drawn in fully and the drawings to become solid structures. The genetic blueprint or nature provides the rough plan; environmental opportunity or nurture enables the structure to be built. Education in its widest sense is the process through which this structure develops.

Movement and Early Learning

The first few years of life are dedicated to gaining control of the body. The human infant is born at a relatively premature stage of development in terms of its motor skills when compared to other land-based mammals, which can get up on to their feet only a few moments after birth. The size of the human brain in relation to the mother's pelvis has meant that the baby must be born at a stage when it can still pass safely through the pelvic bones. The first nine months of postnatal life are in effect the second half of gestation. It is during this time that many of the vital connections are formed between lower and higher centres in the brain, which are necessary for the child to gain muscle strength against gravity, to get up on to its hands and knees, to crawl, and eventually to walk. Once control over the upright posture is established, the hands become free from the task of weight bearing to develop manipulative skills. From then, the child can turn his attention to developing those abilities that are uniquely human – the ability to walk, to talk, and to use symbolic language.

A child gains its first experience of the outside world through movement. During the first 9-12 months of life, the infant will acquire thousands of new movement patterns and movement abilities. At the same time as these movements are being learnt, the infant replicates the brain development of its evolutionary ancestors, passing from the aqueous environment of the womb where movements were fish-like in character, to crawling on its belly like a reptile, creeping on hands and knees like a mammal, 'cruising' on two feet whilst using the hands for support, and eventually gaining confidence and control of balance on two feet.

Figure 1. Characteristics of the movement in the womb – Piscean

Figure 2. Movements characteristic of the first 4-6 months of life – Reptilian

Figure 3. Movements in the quadruped position – Mammalian

Figure 4. From crawling to walking (hands still not entirely free from balance) – Primate

Figure 5. Bipedal – Human

The various stages in motor development reflect development within the brain itself. In the first year of life, the child takes a lightning tour through its own evolutionary heritage in the stages of motor development through which it passes, and the formation of connections within the brain that those movements signify.

How does the young child develop these physical skills?

2. *Balance*

Balance: 'the art of not moving'

Hannah was 12 years old. In her short life she had seen countless experts: a Paediatrician to see if there was any reason why she was late in learning to sit up; a Speech Therapist to investigate delay in learning to talk; an Occupational Therapist to help improve her coordination; and an Educational Psychologist to assess her IQ and find out why she had writing difficulties. All agreed that there was a problem, but Hannah's difficulties did not fit neatly into any recognized category, so she had never been given a diagnosis.

At 12 years of age she had the reading age of a 7 year old and could barely write. She was also emotionally immature and had difficulty making friends. When she came to be assessed, she sat in the corner of the room, bent forwards, her head tucked under one leg, looking at me from under her long blonde fringe. When I asked her if she was comfortable, her father replied, 'Oh yes. She can see you better that way.' When I asked her what happened if she sat up, she said, 'The world turns upside down'.

Further investigations revealed that Hannah had severe problems with balance. Twelve months later, following a year's programme of daily exercises designed to train balance, she sent us a photograph of herself walking along the edge of a canal boat, head held high, laughing. Not only had her balance improved, her perceptual world had stabilized and her reading and writing were catching up with her chronological age. This poses the question, why?

A woman who was in her mid-forties went to a Psychologist because she was severely agoraphobic. Over a number of years, she had found it increasingly difficult to go out by herself. Leaving the house resulted in feelings of acute anxiety and panic, and the only way that she was able go out with any degree of security was to take an old-fashioned flat iron, wrap it in a towel, place it in a plastic bag, and take it with her for a walk. This in itself seemed to be confirmation of her growing neurosis. When the psychologist tested her balance, she fell over. Her 'neurotic' need to take an iron for a walk whenever she left the house was actually fulfilling an important function. It provided a counter-weight to an unidentified problem with balance and allowed her to feel more stable. When her balance disorder was treated, her symptoms of panic, anxiety, and agoraphobia began to subside.

It was the late Paul Schilder's belief, that many of the symptoms of neurosis and psychosis could be traced back to a fault in the functioning of the balance mechanism.

Why is balance so important that dysfunction can result in such a wide variety of symptoms, many of them masquerading as cognitive or emotional disorders?

Balance – the Primary Sense

Balance (the vestibular system) is the oldest of the sensory systems, believed to be some 0.6 billion years old. Hearing, in comparison, is a youngster, having evolved over a mere 0.3 billion years. The task of balance is to facilitate orientation and postural behaviour – the ability of the body to function within the force of gravity, or 'to know your place in space'. This knowledge of place in space provides the primary reference point from which all other spatial judgements and adaptations become possible.[1]

The vestibular system is unique in that it has no special sensation of its own. We are not conscious of balance when it is functioning well and we only become aware of it through the other sensory systems. For example, if we over-stimulate the vestibular system by going on a series of fun-fair rides, we may feel we have left our stomach behind, have 'butterflies', and experience all the excitement that goes with a rush of adrenaline. A rough sea-crossing upsets the relationship between balance, body, and vision, resulting in feelings of motion sickness. In fact, motion sickness is the vestibular system's own form of 'special sickness', indicating that it has fallen out of synchrony with interdependent systems.

If we stand on the edge of a high cliff we might experience vertigo or dizziness. These particular symptoms tell us that the synchrony of signals between the vestibular, visual, and postural systems is disturbed, affecting perception of position in space and influencing many other systems in the body. Hence, Hannah's need to look at me from under her legs so that the world did not turn upside down, and the patient's need to go out with an iron, are not as bizarre as they may seem.

Origins of Balance and Hearing

In terms of evolution, many of our most complex functions have developed over millions of years, through the processes of mutation and salvage of ancient structures that have been adapted into organs of increasing complexity. Hearing developed from the organs of balance, and vision developed from the other two. Balance supports vision by giving stability to the image on the retina despite movement of the head. All three have their origins in the gill bars and intermediate folds of skin found in ancient fish. It is amazing to think that our complex senses of touch, balance, taste, and hearing all have their origins in these ancient structures.

During pregnancy, at circa 21 days of gestation, plaques start to form on the outside of the embryo's head. These plaques are thickenings that will sink into both sides of the head to form hollow cavities, which over the next 30 days will become the inner ear. The cavity then divides to form two interconnected structures. The upper part forms three hollow semi-circular tubes arranged at right angles to each other. These tubes, together with the otolith organs, will become the balance mechanism.

The semi-circular canals detect movement of the head by the motion of fluid inside the tubes, operating like a 'spirit level of the body'.[2] The otolith organs detect information regarding linear movement and static head position. The lower part of the cavity forms a long tube which coils up like a shell to form the cochlea, or hearing apparatus.

The vestibular apparatus begins to send impulses to the developing brain very early in development and will go on to form projections to centres that control posture, body movement, arousal, eye movements, and sensory integration. Balance is also crucial to the efficient functioning of many other processes upon which accurate perception depends.

Balance is not something that we automatically have; it is something that we do. Even walking is a constant process to prevent us from falling over.[3] Balance does not begin when we learn to stand on our two feet toward the end of the first year of life; rather, the upright stance is the product of repeated movement opportunities during the first months of life that have resulted in the development of muscular strength against gravity (tone), and training of balance in many different positions in preparation for upright posture.

Each of the semi-circular canals responds to motion in a different plane in space: one responds to horizontal movement around a vertical axis – movements that involve spinning or turning; another to movement forward and backward through a horizontal axis – rocking, swinging, seesaws etc.; the third responds to motion that involves tilting movements such as standing on a board that wobbles from side to side, being in an aeroplane that 'banks' as it changes course, or on a boat on a windy day. The latter is the plane that is stimulated least during the course of everyday life, and is the one that causes most problems if stimulated suddenly – hence the experience of being seasick or airsick, despite being a good traveller on land.

Development of Balance

'Myelination' refers to the neurological equivalent of insulating an electrical circuit – nerve fibres are covered in a fatty sheath which helps transmission of messages along that circuit to be more efficient, and reduces interference or 'cross talk' from other pathways. Although the balance mechanism is the first fibre tract in the brain to begin myelinating and is more mature than any of the other sensory systems before birth, while still in the womb the foetus has been suspended in an aqueous environment, carried through space by the mother and cushioned from the full force of gravity. From the moment of birth, a baby must learn to develop its own abilities within this force. This requires the development of muscle tone, postural control, and cooperation with the other senses. Vision and balance must learn to work together; hearing must learn to support balance in helping the baby to locate sound in the environment (orientation to outside stimuli); touch and muscular awareness (kinesthesis) will eventually help the infant to have an inner

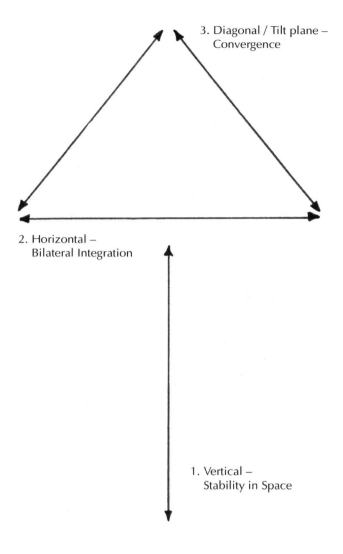

Figure 6. The three planes of gravity/axes for operations in space

awareness of its place in space, but none can work their magic in isolation. All must act in cooperation with the vestibular system.

The vestibular system may be the expert *in* movement, but it receives its training *through* movement. When we try a new skill for the first time, our efforts are often clumsy. Hopefully, with practice we improve, but in our early attempts our movements are usually poorly controlled, overshoot the target, and deteriorate if we have to slow down for any reason. Do you remember learning to ride a bicycle for the first time? Once movement started you were lulled into a temporary state of security as motion enabled you to maintain your balance. As soon as you had to slow down, wobble would set in, steering might veer to one side, and you probably needed to use one of your feet for support.

Balance through Movement – Vital Training

Babies develop motor control in much the same way. Their earliest movements are uncontrolled, but the more they move, the better control becomes. The development of reaching is a prime example of this. At first, the baby will swipe at the desired object, either missing the target entirely or knocking it over. It will repeat the swiping motion many times before it can approach the object with accuracy, starting with large circular movements and gradually refining them so that it can go straight to the desired object. Practice is therefore an essential ingredient of every child's play, and the best place to start practising balance is in space.

A baby's first playground is the floor. Lying on its back and kicking its legs, it learns to feel, as a result of movement, how long it is. By waving and spreading its arms, it starts to know how wide it is – this is called *proprioceptive learning*, or knowledge of the inner self, which is gained directly as a result of movement experience. When lying on the tummy, a baby learns to hold its head up; a few weeks later it will start to support some of its weight on the forearms, whilst tactile contact with the ground, supporting of body weight and gathering muscle strength, all help to develop the compound sense of body map.

Secure balance is inseparable from the development of postural control, which in turn is supported by information from the visual, proprioceptive, and motor systems. Training of these systems is a gradual process during which maturation of the vestibular pathways involved will take until at least 7 years of age, and continue through puberty and beyond. Immature vestibular functioning is frequently found amongst children who have specific learning difficulties such as Dyslexia and Dyspraxia, problems of attention, language impairment, emotional problems, and adults who suffer from anxiety, Agoraphobia and Panic Disorder.[4]

A Sense of Direction

Balance supplies the brain with information regarding body position in space. This information gives a child its sense of 'centre' in space, described by A. Jean Ayres as 'gravitational security'. Knowledge of one's own position in space is essential for orientation, directional awareness, and effective operations in space.

Imagine being given a map and being told to find your way to point B without knowing where you are. Navigation requires knowledge of your own position before you can find your way to other points on the map. Levinson (1984) likened the balance system to an internal compass system, which 'reflexively tells us spatial relationships such as right and left, up and down, front and back, east and west and north and south'.

Balance and Learning

Higher cognitive skills such as reading and writing, which require directional awareness (why else should you write 'was' rather than 'saw', or 'on' as opposed to 'no'?), depend upon stable balance to underpin accurate left-to-right and right-to-left directional awareness. Similarly, in order to tell the time, we need to know the difference between left and right, up and down, before and after. This ability begins with knowledge of one's own position in space. Children who continue to reverse letters, numbers, and words after the age of 8 years are also often found to have immature balance.[5]

The vestibular system can also have a profound effect upon emotions. It is linked (via the Reticular Activating System, or RAS) to the limbic system. The limbic system, which humans share in common with other mammals, is that part of the brain where raw feelings, instincts, and emotions are processed and generated. Over-active (hyper) or under-active (hypo) vestibular functioning can result in over- or under-arousal of the limbic system, which will respond by alerting either the sympathetic ('fight or flight' reaction) or parasympathetic (slows down basic functions such as heart rate) divisions of the autonomic nervous system. Either division elicits specific physiological and biochemical changes in the body that are associated with different types of physiological and emotional experience.

Vestibular stimulation can have an impact on learning in several ways:

1. Maturation of vestibular pathways helps to develop inhibitory mechanisms as a result of habituation.
2. It helps to improve postural reactions that are inseparable from balance.
3. It promotes better integration of the different sensory systems.
4. It improves stability of retinal image as a result of maturation of the vestibular-ocular-reflex (VOR), thereby providing a basis for stable eye movements.

How is Balance Trained?

Mothers have known instinctively since time immemorial that slow movement has a calming effect and that rapid movement increases arousal or excitement. She will soothe a fretful baby by holding it in her arms and gently rocking from side to side. Swinging cradles and rocking chairs furnished the nurseries of old because gentle vestibular stimulation helped to lull the baby to sleep. Lullabies such as 'Rock-a-bye, baby, on the tree top' all follow a side-to-side rocking rhythm. The rocking chair was also a favourite with Granny because rocking motion helps to relieve pressure on aching joints and provides vestibular stimulation to a body that has limited mobility. Several studies[6] have shown that children who are given regular vestibular stimulation in the first months of life show accelerated development in motor skills, while at the other end of life, one of the first signs of brain degeneration is when balance starts to deteriorate.

Rapid vestibular stimulation is a part of normal playfulness or rough-and-tumble play. Parents have played such games with their children for centuries – 'down in the deep blue sea' and 'this is the way the ladies ride'. Games that involve 'throwing' the child in the air will elicit squeals of delight, but these are not games to play just before bedtime if you want your child to go straight to sleep! Playground equipment such as carousels, slides, swings, and see-saws are designed to 'work' the balance mechanism. Young children do not get dizzy as adults do, because connections between balance and other centres are still being formed in the first eight years of life. During these early years, movement opportunity is definitely food for the brain.

Types of movements that help to train balance involve changes of movement in space:

1. Up and down movements – such as jumping, trampolining, playing on a bouncy castle, or going down a slide.

2. To and fro – such as running, starting and stopping, and swinging.
3. Centrifugal force – carousels.
4. Turning movements of the body – movements used in spinning, dancing, rolling, or turning somersaults.
5. Depth – riding on a scooter-board.

Some signs and symptoms which might indicate balance problems are:

- Breech presentation;
- Delay in achieving head control and other dependent milestones such as sitting, crawling, and walking;
- Poorly developed muscle tone;
- Frequent falls;
- Avoidance/fear of movement;
- Clumsiness – dropping or knocking things;
- No fear of heights (under-active vestibular system);
- Excessive fear of heights (hypersensitive vestibular functioning);
- Excessive rocking or spinning (attempt to provide stimulation to an under-active system);
- Poorly developed sense of body image – tendency to move too close to other people, accidents with other children in playground etc.;
- Doesn't know 'how' – push or pull actions? Difficulty modelling or initiating certain types of movement;
- Motion sickness above the age of 8 years;
- Difficulty learning to ride a bicycle;
- Inability mentally to rotate or reverse objects in space, e.g. learning to read a clock.

3. Brain and Body – Developing the Mind

> 'In the first 5 years of life, the child is father to the man he will come to be.'
>
> Arnold Gesell (1984)

The brain of a new-born baby already contains nearly all of the brain cells that it will need throughout the rest of life, even though it is only about one third of the size of the adult brain. The main period of brain growth occurs in the first year of life, although fine structural changes will continue into adulthood. Of the 100 billion cells that are present at birth, only a fraction of this number will actually be used during the span of its life. Between 15 months and 6 years of age, the cerebral cortex appears to double in size, with synaptic density (a synapse being the point of communication between two adjacent nerve cells) reaching its peak at about 3-$3^{1}/_{2}$ years of age, a level 50 per cent higher than it was at birth, or will be at puberty.

In the beginning, neurons are unspecialized – not 'primed' for any particular function. This is known as 'equal potential', meaning flexibility of function. During the course of development, constant interaction with the environment or experience stimulates the formation of connections within the brain, particularly connections to higher or 'executive' centres that will eventually command the whole. The first years of life are the time for structuring and organizing these connections.

As neurons migrate, so they become more specialized in their function. In the course of the first three years of life, the brain forms almost twice as many synapses (junctions) than it will actually use. Those that are in constant use will strengthen to form the motorways of the mind; those that are unused will either be replaced by others or will eventually disappear. During infancy, many neurons retain flexibility of function or neural 'plasticity'. In this sense, every human being is truly unique. Experience shapes the architecture of the brain but no two people ever receive exactly the same experience even if the genetic blueprint is identical, as in the case of identical twins. Experiences may be similar, but position, timing, and perspective will always be slightly different, creating a neuronal tapestry that cannot be precisely replicated in any way.

There are several stages in development when the brain goes through a period of neural housekeeping, when inactive or redundant cells are 'pruned' in a spring-cleaning exercise which sweeps away neural clutter and strengthens connections that are in frequent use. One such spring-cleaning period occurs between $6^{1}/_{2}$ and 8 years of age, and another during the teenage years, so that by the late teen years only half of the synapses that were present in the three year old will remain. It is perhaps not surprising that the adolescent years are frequently described as ones of turmoil. One scientific magazine recently described the teenager's brain as being like, 'a building site under construction'. Many parents will identify their teenager's bedroom as reflecting this apparently chaotic state of reorganization.

Such vigorous pruning has both advantages and disadvantages. By removing excess pathways, interference or cross-chatter is reduced, allowing for greater efficiency of functioning. On the other hand, connections between neurons and their target cells in pathways that have not been used become weaker over time. This is sometimes described as 'neuronal fitness'. Fitness of neurons is determined by success in establishing contact with other cells and passing information. Something in the process of making contact helps to protect neurons from destruction – a neurological explanation for the old adage, 'use it or lose it'.

Developmental changes in cognition and behaviour are associated with changes in the brain and vice-versa. When looking at a child's capacity for learning, we cannot separate learning from development, or development from the structure and activity of the brain. During development, the structure undergoes continuous change. Nature and nurture act as twin sculptors in this process. Capacity for language acquisition provides one such example.

At birth, a baby's hearing is open to a wide range of sound frequencies – frequencies that cover the spectrum of all the languages under the sun. If the child has the opportunity to hear and start to utter the sounds of those languages in the first three years of life, the ability to hear and pronounce the sounds will remain, provided they are used. As the infant 'tunes in' to the sounds of his/her mother tongue, discrimination within a very specific band of frequencies improves at the expense of those frequencies that are not required. If a child needs to learn a new language at a later age, the neurons that might have become specialized for that language may have become specialized for a different function or simply have been discarded as redundant. New languages can be learned, but accent and fluency will never be acquired with such consummate ease again.

Motor Development

In the new-born, the most active parts of the brain are the regions that govern immediate survival: breathing, heart rate, and reflexes. These survival functions are controlled from the brain-stem, the primitive part of the brain, which is shared by man, mammal, and reptile. Higher regions of the brain mature at different rates, but the first area to mature is the motor area, followed by the sensory area and eventually the association area. The latter continues to mature into the 20s and 30s, but in early development, survival functions take priority.

Reflexes – Signposts of Development

The earliest movements of the embryo are intrinsic and spontaneous. It is thought that these random movements are instigated by the activity of motor neurons and inter-neurons. These early movements are natural impulses and are not just simple responses to sensory stimuli.

The first signs of *response* to sensory signals are seen through a series of reflexes that support the developing child until such time as it gains a degree of voluntary control over specific functions.

Reflexes are innate stereotyped responses to specific stimuli. There are three groups of reflexes, which support the child through its first $3^{1}/_{2}$ years of life:

1. **Intra-Uterine Reflexes** – reflexes that emerge in the womb starting at just $5^{1}/_{2}$ to 7 weeks after conception. Many of the intra-uterine reflexes are inhibited (controlled) during uterine life, although some of them remain present for a short time after birth. The characteristic of the intra-uterine reflexes is a 'withdrawal' from noxious stimuli. Simple withdrawal reactions are characteristic of primitive organisms that do not

possess more complex reaction patterns. They are in essence a defensive reaction and are mediated at the level where the brain links through to the spinal cord – the spinal level.

2. **Primitive Reflexes** – reflexes that start to emerge in the womb. The first primitive reflex to appear is the Moro reflex at 9-12 weeks after conception. Primitive reflexes should be fully developed in the full-term baby (40 weeks gestation). They are thought to assist the baby in the process of being born, and support survival during the first weeks of life before connections to higher centres in the brain have been established. They also provide rudimentary training for later voluntary skills. Primitive reflexes are inhibited by the developing brain by 6-12 months of life. They are mediated at the level of the brain stem.

3. **Postural Reflexes** – reflexes that start to emerge shortly after birth and continue to develop up to $3^{1}/_{2}$ years of age. Once established, the postural reflexes should remain for life. These reflexes are controlled at the level of the midbrain and the cerebellum, with the exception of one postural reflex involved in the control of eye movements which is mediated from the cortex.

In the transition from early reflexes to later reactions, evolving control of higher brain centres over lower ones is revealed.

If there is accident or injury to higher centres in the brain, postural reflexes may cease to function, and primitive reflexes will re-emerge. This situation is seen in certain degenerative diseases such as Multiple Sclerosis when demyelination destroys the efficient functioning of specific pathways, and in Alzheimer's disease when destruction of higher brain centres results in the release of earlier, more primitive patterns of response. (Myelination, it will be

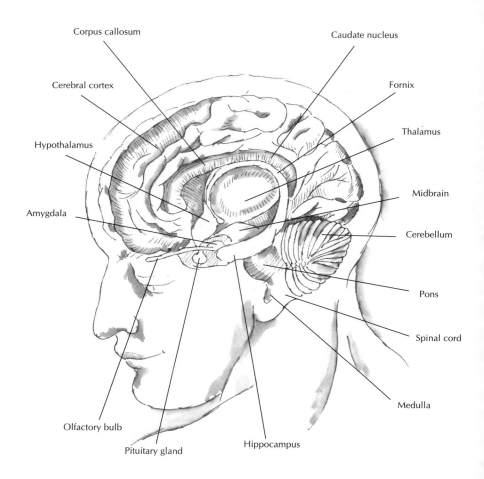

Figure 7. Hierarchical view of the brain (The Evolutionary Brain)

recalled, is the process by which nerve fibres are coated in a fatty sheath which permits more efficient transmission of information along that fibre.) Certain types of brain injury at birth, such as cerebral palsy, can affect the development of the central nervous system so that the primitive reflexes never come under the full control of the cortex, remaining active into later life and interfering with smooth motor control and motor dependent functions.

In the young baby, reflexes form part of its natural repertoire of communication with the outside world. In the last three months of pregnancy, reflexes have helped the foetus to turn, to kick, to move its arms and legs, and even to suck its thumb. A well-developed suck reflex is going to be important for feeding as soon as the baby is born. In the weeks leading up to birth, the foetus can open and close its eyes in preparation for blinking; it can respond to sound, and during periods of rapid-eye-movement sleep, it practises breathing movements.

The foetus is also often wiser than the adult. When it has the maturity to survive outside of the womb, it releases a hormone into the mother's bloodstream that triggers the onset of labour. Reflexes should help mother and baby to work together as cooperative partners during the birth process so that the reflexes are both utilized and strengthened during a normal vaginal delivery. If the birth process is prolonged or difficult, artificially induced, or involves obstetric intervention such as forceps delivery or Caesarean section, these normal processes are by-passed and can sometimes have an impact on later reflex development.

Functions of Reflexes in Early Development

Reflexes are the primary teachers of basic motor skills. By providing an innate response to key stimuli they facilitate a specific motor response to specific sensory stimuli. The more a child moves, the better his control over movement becomes. Each time he flexes or wiggles his toes, kicks his legs, or reaches with his arm, motor cells begin a process of modification, which become more definite and permanent with repetition. These modifications will eventually culminate in walking and stable balance on two feet. Increased control of movement is indicative of strengthening connections between the brain and the body and within the brain itself. In this way, movement helps to map the brain, and the reflexes provide a child with his earliest vocabulary of movement.

An understanding of what reflexes do in early development, and of their impact if they fail to be integrated during the early years of life, is useful in order to understand why movement is so vital for learning, and also how the reflexes themselves can be used as signposts of development.

The history of a child's early development can be read through its postural abilities at a later age. The human being is eternally fascinated by events that have occurred outside of conscious memory. Life before birth and in the first three years of life – the years before verbal language (and conscious memory) is established – provide just such an enigma. Many of those memories are hidden and held within the postural, motor, and sensory capabilities of the child – the early building blocks of later language and the containers of emotion. The body holds within it the secrets of many of those pre-conscious memories.

4. From Cradle to Coordination: Reflexes and the Developing Mind

> 'Reflex action is the deputy of the brain, and directs myriad movements, thus leaving the higher powers free to attend to weightier things.'
>
> Halleck, 1898

The Moro Reflex

The Moro reflex is the first of the primitive reflexes to emerge at between 9 and 12 weeks after conception. It continues to develop through pregnancy and should be present in the full-term infant (40 weeks gestation). Named 'Umklammerung reflex' by Moro, meaning the 'clasping reflex', it describes the infant's response to any sudden unexpected event, particularly loss of head support.

If the baby's head is lowered rapidly below the level of the spine, the arms and legs will open out from the characteristic flexed posture of the new-born, there will be a rapid intake of breath, and the baby will 'freeze' in that position for a fraction of second, before the arms and legs return across the body, usually accompanied by a cry of protest.

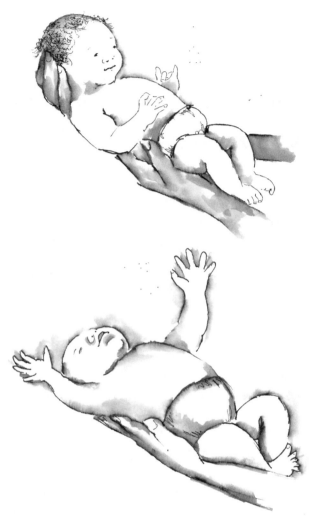

Figures 8 and 9. The Moro Reflex

The Moro reflex provides an instantaneous arousal mechanism, activating the primitive fight/flight reaction and also stimulating the breathing centre in the brain. During a normal delivery, each contraction exerts pressure on the chest cavity. Gentle rhythmic chest compression helps to rid the lungs of fluid in preparation for breathing after birth. Oxygen supply to the brain is reduced, resulting in a *mild* degree of hypoxia (oxygen deprivation), which primes the breathing centre in the brain in preparation for breathing air. At the moment of birth for a healthy baby, when compression is released it acts rather like the recoil of an elastic band, pushing air into the lungs as the baby takes its first breath. If this fails to occur spontaneously, nature seems to have provided a second fail-safe mechanism – the Moro reflex. The Moro reflex can be activated by appropriate stimulation of any one of the sensory systems and should, except in cases of sick or traumatized babies, be sufficient to stimulate the first intake of breath.

By four months of age the Moro reaction should be modified so that if there is a sudden or unexpected event, the baby 'startles', raises its shoulders, and starts to search the environment to seek out the source of danger (orientation). Provided the infant has the means to cope with the source of alert, it will either respond to it (attention), or ignore it (filter unwanted stimuli out of conscious awareness). This later reaction pattern forms the basis of the adult startle response, and indicates increased maturity within the nervous system as well as forming a basis for selective attention.

If the Moro reflex persists beyond its normal period of activity (four months of life), it is associated with increased sensitivity and reactivity to sudden unexpected stimuli. Sudden loss of balance, postural instability, or unexpected stimulation of any one of the senses can release the Moro reflex from cortical control. This is important because the Moro reflex does not allow time for the *conscious* brain to analyse the situation and direct an appropriate response. Instead, the system goes into emergency mode as the Moro reflex acts as the primitive 'fight or flight' reaction. In other words, the child reacts first, and thinks afterwards – a major ingredient of impulsive and inappropriate behaviour.

The Moro reflex is particularly significant because it can be activated by any one of the sensory systems, although after birth it is most sensitive to over-stimulation of the balance mechanism and sudden loud noise.[7]

Functions of the Moro Reflex

• Primitive reaction to change of position, or balance before higher systems of control have become available;
• May assist in taking the first breath of life;
• Activates the fight/flight response;
• To alert, arouse, and summon assistance.

The Moro reflex can be activated by:

1. Sudden change of head or body position (vestibular/postural)
2. Sudden change of light (visual)
3. Sudden loud noise (auditory)
4. Sudden change of temperature or pain (tactile)
5. Smoke (olfactory)

A strongly retained Moro reflex is often seen in cases of cerebral palsy, but traces of the Moro reflex can also persist in the absence of identified pathology. In the latter case, it is associated with a variety of symptoms that can continue to have an effect upon later development.

Symptoms associated with a Residual Moro Reflex

• Hypersensitivity and over-reactivity to certain stimuli;
• Vestibular-related problems such as motion sickness, which continues beyond puberty;
• Poor balance and coordination;

- Difficulty catching a ball or processing rapidly approaching visual stimuli;
- Immature eye movements and visual perceptual abilities, particularly stimulus-bound effect (the inability to ignore irrelevant visual information within a given visual field). This can result in difficulty sustaining visual attention and high distractibility;
- Insecurity;
- Generalized anxiety and/or fearfulness;
- Dislike of sudden unexpected events, e.g. loud noises, bright lights;
- Poor adaptability and dislike of change.

These are the children who tend to cling to familiarity, dislike change, and often attempt to manipulate people and situations in order to maintain a modicum of control. They are often highly intelligent, but find it difficult to respond appropriately when a rapid response is required. A discrepancy between verbal and emotional and social behaviour often exists, causing problems with peer relationships. The Moro-driven child can appear withdrawn and fearful in social situations or have a tendency to be overbearing and controlling. They are frequently the children who are 'picked on' in the playground because other children recognize their weaknesses and their tendency to over-react to stressful situations. The Moro reflex is sometimes seen in adults who suffer from anxiety and panic disorder.[8]

The Tonic Labyrinthine Reflex (TLR)

This is a reflex response to change of head position forward or backward through the mid-plane. If a baby is held supported on its back in an adult's hands, and the head is lowered below the level of the spine, the baby's arms and legs straighten.

Figure 10. The Tonic Labyrinthine Reflex (TLR) Extension

If the head is raised above the level of the spine, the arms and legs flex and the baby curls up into a position similar to the one characteristically adopted in the womb – the position known as 'flexor habitus'.

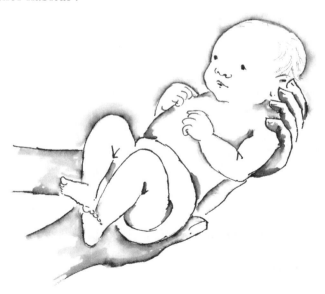

Figure 11. The Tonic Labyrinthine Reflex (TLR) Flexion

In the first few weeks of life, the TLR is the baby's only way of responding to gravity. It has not yet developed the neck- and head-righting reactions necessary to hold its head up, and unless the head is supported, muscle tone will be either predominantly extensor (rigid) or flexed (floppy).

In the first few weeks after birth, the baby makes remarkably rapid progress in gaining some degree of control over the TLR. By just six weeks of age, it learns to hold its head up in line with the spine if placed on the tummy.

Figure12. Early attempts at head righting in the prone position

This is a first step toward gaining control over the neck muscles, which will provide the basis for upper-trunk control and eventually normal distribution of muscle tone throughout the body irrespective of head position. This mastery of head control is fundamental to later balance, posture, and coordination.

Normal development begins in a head-to-toe (cephalo-caudal) and centre-outwards (proximo-distal) sequence. In other words, *the first lesson a child must learn is control of the head position on the body.* Correct head alignment provides the balance mechanism located deep inside the inner ear, with a reference point from

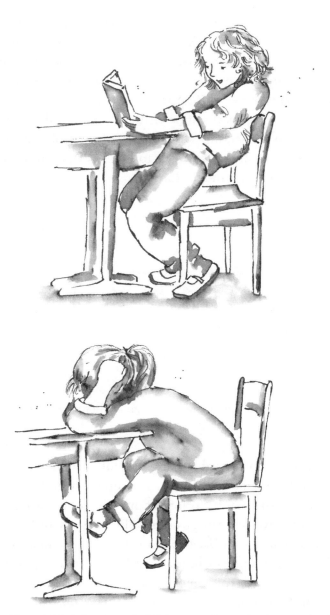

Figures 13 and 14. School aged child attempting to 'accommodate' the effect of a residual tonic labyrinthine reflex (TLR) when sitting which it can direct other muscle groups and systems such as vision, to work together in maintaining balance and postural control.

Head control develops first from lying on the tummy, followed a few weeks later when lying on the back. It is important for a baby to have plenty of opportunity for freedom of movement in both positions if it is to gain good head control in the horizontal plane. This control will then be challenged as the movement and postural capabilities of the child increase to include, rolling, crawling on the stomach, sitting (semi-upright), creeping on hands and knees, and eventually standing and walking (vertical). As later righting and equilibrium reactions replace primitive reflexes, balance becomes more stable; muscle tone improves and reaches into the highest levels of function. 'It becomes part and parcel of postural manipulative behaviour, including the adjustments of oculo-motor and laryngeal muscles. Organised tonus is the living framework of voluntary movement and acts of attention.' [9]

It takes up to 3-3$\frac{1}{2}$ years of age for the TLR to be fully inhibited by higher centres in the brain, indicating just how *many* stages and skills need to be layered one upon the other before control of balance and tonus become established. You only have to watch a baby taking its first steps – wide gait, arms in the air, lurching forward and staggering from one foot to the other – to recognize how precarious is the human relationship with gravity. Initially each step is taken to stop itself from falling over. This is a major discovery: that by putting one foot in front of the other, effective locomotion results; that the view of the world is better; and that once balance is mastered, the hands also become free, opening up all sorts of possibilities for further exploration and development. But the beginning of upright balance starts on the tummy. All animate forms of locomotion from the worm to the antelope start in a prone relationship with gravity.

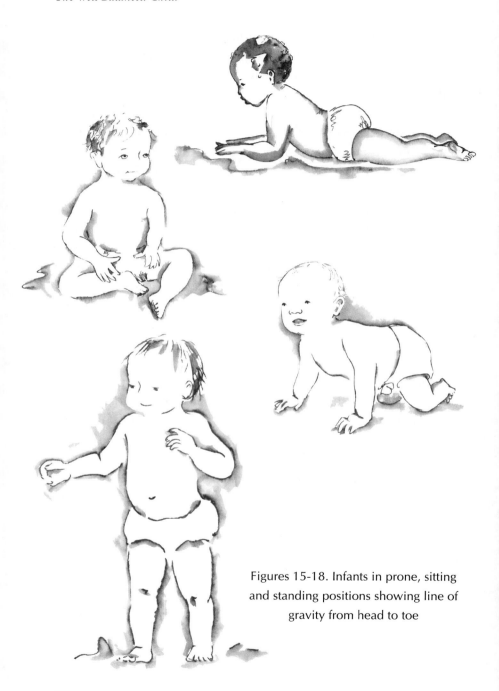

Figures 15-18. Infants in prone, sitting and standing positions showing line of gravity from head to toe

Functions of the Tonic Labyrinthine Reflex

• Primitive reaction to alteration of head position through the mid-plane;

• Facilitates contraction and extension of major muscle groups to develop muscle tone and muscular control;

• Facilitates the beginning of extensor muscle tone (by helping to straighten the baby out from the curled-up foetal position adopted inside the womb);

• Interacts with a series of other reflexes and reactions over the course of the first $3^{1}/_{2}$ years of life to provide the basis for head control, balance, postural stability, and other dependent functions.

Like the Moro reflex, the TLR has a natural obsolescence. As movement capabilities increase and later reflexes develop, the TLR is gradually modified so that by $3^{1}/_{2}$ years of age, higher systems gain control and the TLR can be inhibited, only to be called upon if accident, injury, or extreme circumstances arise. If, for any reason, later reflexes do not develop properly, traces of the TLR can remain active in the older child and have an adverse effect upon basic motor abilities.

Effects of a Retained Tonic Labyrinthine Reflex

• Postural instability arising from head position or movement through the mid-plane, which then has an effect upon –
    ♦ Balance
    ♦ Muscle tone
• Timing of signals from the body to the balance system and related circuits such as centres involved in the control of eye movements.

Symptoms of a Retained Tonic Labyrinthine Reflex

- Poor balance
- Postural problems
- Walking on the toes (after the age of $3^{1}/_{2}$)
- Floppy or 'tight' muscle tone
- Control of eye movements
- Visual-perceptual problems
- Vertigo
- Motion sickness which continues beyond puberty
- Orientation and auditory confusion

The Asymmetrical Tonic Neck Reflex (ATNR)

As its name implies, the Asymmetrical Tonic Neck Reflex affects muscle tone differently on each side of the body, in response to turning of the head to either side. The reflex starts to emerge approximately 18 weeks after conception, at about the same time as the expectant mother starts to feel her baby's movements for the first time.

When the baby turns the head to one side, the arm and leg extend in the same direction as the head movement, and the opposite limbs flex. This movement should increase in strength during pregnancy, helping to develop movement, particularly turning movements in the confines of the womb and muscle tone.

It has been suggested that the ATNR, together with other reflexes, helps in the birth process. In a normal presentation, between 32 and 34 weeks, the baby turns to position itself with the head facing down toward the mother's pelvis. The presentation of the baby refers to the part of the baby that overlies the entrance to the birth canal at the brim of the pelvis. In this position, the head is bent forward with the chin resting on

Figure 19. The Asymmetrical Tonic Neck Reflex (ATNR)

the chest, the arms crossed, the legs bent at the knee, and the feet crossed over the genitalia. The ideal position for both mother and baby at the onset of labour is for the baby to lie with its back facing to the front of the mother's abdomen in an 'anterior' position, with the baby well flexed and the head placed over the pelvic brim ready to engage.

As labour proceeds, the baby is not only pushed slowly down the birth canal as a result of maternal contractions alone, but must also perform a 180° turn, moving down the birth canal in a slow spiral. This turn is necessary for the baby to ease its way through the tight dimensions of the mother's pelvis relative to the baby's own head size. The average pelvic opening in human females is 13 centimetres at its largest diameter and 10 centimetres at its smallest. The average infant head is 10 centimetres front to back, and the shoulders are 12 centimetres across.[10] The widest part of the birth canal is from side to side, but this changes half way down so that the long axis of the oval extends from the front of the mother's body to her back. In order for the largest parts of the baby to be aligned with the accommodating parts of the mother, the baby must carry out a sequence of turns. Several reflexes help the baby to do just this: the ATNR by giving flexibility to the shoulders and the hips as pressure is exerted on the neck, and the Spinal Galant and Perez reflexes by responding to pressure exerted by the vaginal wall on the lumbar region. The Spinal Galant facilitates movement of one hip, while the Perez reflex results in a forward-backward thrust of the lower part of the spine. If the birth was very rapid (precipitate) or the baby became 'stuck' in the birth canal and obstetric intervention such as forceps, ventouse extraction, or emergency Caesarean Section was required, it is possible that either the ATNR was not strong enough, or the position of the baby prevented it from being utilized effectively. This can have implications for the ATNR later in development.

In the first few weeks of life, the ATNR can readily be seen when the baby turns its head to one side. If the baby is placed on its tummy, the ATNR should come into action so that the head automatically turns to one side, thereby ensuring that the airway is free. When asleep on the back, the baby will often adopt an ATNR attitude. Inhibition of the ATNR is a gradual process that undergoes progressive change with increased maturity and acquisition of other abilities related to posture, tone, and bilateral integration (use of the two sides of the body together).

At birth, the neonate is very short-sighted and can only focus at a distance of some 12-17 centimetres from the face – the same visual distance that is used when feeding. The new-born is not aware that its hands are part of itself. Movement that takes place within its limited visual field, such as movement of its own hands, fascinates it. As long as the ATNR is active, head rotation results in extension of the arm, with the eyes following the fingers in the same direction. The baby is not yet aware that the moving toys in front of her face (her own hands) are actually a part of herself; they come and go as she moves her head from side to side. In other words, eyes, hand, and head are all locked together into a single movement. This movement places the hand in a new position from which it can be viewed, and helps to extend the baby's focusing distance from near-point to arm's length.

Within a short period of time, the hand will come into contact with solid objects, enabling the baby to feel and see how far the object is away from it. Movement, vision, and touch thus combine together to sow the early seeds for accommodation – the ability to focus the eyes at different distances. Early attempts at reaching are also helped by the ATNR. As the ATNR is inhibited (circa six months of age), eye and hand movements become increasingly free from head movement. This sequence of events has led a number of authors to observe that the ATNR provides the first hand-eye coordination training in the early weeks and months of life.[11,12]

Inhibition of the ATNR results in less asymmetrical distribution of muscle tone. The baby can start to bring its hands to the midline; and eye movements can start to operate independently of head movement, which results in greater stability of visual image on the retina. This is important in order to be able visually to 'fixate' on an object despite movement of the self or the environment.

Although the ATNR is inhibited in its crude form around six months of age, it remains present as an 'attitudinal' reflex into later life, so that if balance or posture becomes insecure, the ATNR will temporarily reappear until balance is restored. This can be seen at various stages of motor development, when the child acquires a new postural ability such as sitting or standing:

the ATNR may re-emerge for a short period of time until stability and confidence in the new-found skill is established.

Sometimes in adult life, the ATNR is intentionally released from cortical control to assist in the execution of specific skills that involve shifting of balance to one side. Fukuda[13] demonstrated the ATNR being deliberately accessed by a ballerina, a pole-vaulter, and an archer, who enrol the ATNR to affect an 'attitude'. Such examples show that although reflexes become integrated during the course of normal development, they never entirely go away. They can be called upon at any time to enhance performance, or as a last line of defence when the centre of balance is shifted.

Functions of the Asymmetrical Tonic Neck Reflex

- Facilitate movement and exercise muscles in the womb
- Assist in the birth process
- Turn the head to one side so that breathing can take place when lying on the tummy (new-born)
- Develop homolateral (one-sided) movements, which help to break up the total body movement patterns seen in the new-born
- Develop early hand-eye coordination
- Facilitate early reaching movements

Effects of a Retained Asymmetrical Tonic Neck Reflex

Sometimes the ATNR fails to be inhibited by higher centres in the brain in the first year of life. In contrast to the ballerina or the pole-vaulter who *choose* to utilize the ATNR in order to carry out a particular movement (voluntary selection), the ATNR *imposes* itself on other movements when the head is turned to one side (involuntary control). This can interfere with the development of balance and coordination in various ways:

- Problems crossing the midline of the body if the head is turned to one side, affecting
  1. development of cross-pattern movements
  2. crawling on the stomach
  3. bilateral integration
  4. establishment of laterality (preferred side) by 8 years of age
- Development of independent eye movements (the head and eyes still want to move together). This can then have an effect on visual tracking at a later age, which is necessary for reading and writing.

The Symmetrical Tonic Neck Reflex (STNR)

The Symmetrical Tonic Neck Reflex is present for a short period of time immediately after birth. It disappears, only to re-emerge at 6-9 months of age and then to be inhibited at 9-11 months of life. Unlike the TLR, which resulted in total flexion or extension of muscle groups throughout the body as a result of head movement through the mid-plane, the STNR causes upper and lower sections of the body to perform *opposite* movements. It reappears just *before* a baby is ready to get up on to hands and knees to creep on all fours. However, each time the baby puts its head down, the arms bend and the legs try to straighten.

Figure 20. The Symmetrical Tonic Neck Reflex (STNR) in Flexion

If the baby puts its head up, the arms straighten, the legs bend, and the bottom sinks back on to the ankles.

Figure 21. The Symmetrical Tonic Neck Reflex (STNR) in Extension

As long as this occurs, the baby is unable to get upper and lower sections of the body to cooperate in maintaining a stable four-point kneeling position, which is necessary for creeping on hands and knees.

Most babies pass through a phase of rocking on hands and knees, often learning how to move backward before they are able to creep forward. In learning to support its weight on hands and knees, the baby has presented the balance mechanism with an entirely new orientation to gravity. The motion of rocking helps the balance and muscular systems in the upper and lower halves of the body to operate together more efficiently in order to maintain a stable posture. From this position, new movement possibilities become available.

The creeping stage of development is important in itself. Weight bearing on the hands and knees helps to align the upper and lower ends of the spine in preparation for standing up and walking. Vision, proprioception and balance learn how to operate together in a new relationship with gravity, and the hand-eye coordination that takes place when creeping occurs at the same visual distance that the child will use some years later when reading and writing.

Figures 22 and 23. Sitting positions typical of an older child with a Symmetrical Tonic Neck Reflex (STNR)

It has been observed that many children who later experience difficulties with reading and writing did not crawl or creep in the first year of life. This has sometimes been suggested as a possible cause of specific learning difficulties, but there are also other children who did not crawl or creep and who do not experience any later learning problems. If ATNR and STNR were still active at the time when a child would naturally have learned how to crawl, they can prevent the baby from being able to coordinate the necessary movements – in these cases, later learning difficulties seem to follow. Other children simply pass from crawling to standing and walking without ill-effect. The important point is to allow your baby to experience as wide a range of movements as possible; to enjoy and value each stage of development as it occurs – *not to try to push your child on to the next stage before it is ready to move on by itself.*

In development, the most important changes often start to take place before they can actually be seen, rather like seeds germinating beneath the ground. By the time a new developmental skill is evident, like seedlings emerging in the Spring, much of the organization, which is necessary for the skill to develop, has already taken place. The period of development that occurs 'in the dark' is as important as the practice of that new skill when it actually emerges. Pushing a child toward a new skill too soon can cut short the preceding period of organization and preparation, which provides the basis for later automatization of functioning.

Functions of the Symmetrical Tonic Neck Reflex

- To help the baby get up off the ground;
- To align the pelvic and occipital (back of the head) regions of the spine in preparation for the upright stance;
- To break up the total flexion/extension pattern dictated by the TLR;
- To help train visual adjustment from near to far distance.

In common with other primitive reflexes, if the STNR remains active for too long it can interfere with the development of other skills. The child will have difficulty maintaining certain positions because the upper and lower sections of the body are at odds with each other. This is most noticeable in the older child when sitting at a table to write or to eat a meal. If the child looks down, the arms bend, making it difficult to maintain an upright sitting posture and write at the same time.

Bringing the hand toward the mouth can also be difficult because change in head position affects muscle tone in both of the arms, interfering with control of speed and coordination of arm movement. These are the children who continue to be messy eaters long after other children seem to have mastered using a spoon or knife and fork. They also have difficulty in learning to swim because the upper and lower parts of the body do not want to work together to keep the body level. (Some children learn to swim under water first, because the weight of the water helps to keep the two halves of the body aligned.) Children who have a strong STNR at a later age often appear to be lazy or 'slothful'. Lacking appropriate distribution of muscle tone as an opposing force to the constant pull of gravity, they struggle to maintain upright posture, and experience real discomfort when sitting or standing. Everything that they do seems to require extra effort, and they are often the children of whom teachers and parents complain that 'they won't sit still!'.

Observations of children who had difficulty staying still led two former professors of English at the University of Indianapolis, O'Dell and Cook, to set up the Bender Institute. In the 1970s Miriam Bender, an occupational therapist, published her doctoral thesis in which she had compared the incidence of a retained STNR in a group of learning-disabled children with a group of children without learning problems. She found that the STNR was present in 75 per cent of the learning-disabled group, but not evident in any of the others. When, in the year 2000, I carried out a study looking at the incidence of a cluster of abnormal reflexes in a group of 54 children who had been diagnosed with dyslexia, I found the STNR to be present in 73 per cent of the group.[14] Miriam Bender then developed a series of physical exercises that involved creeping against an opposing force. She found that the exercises had an inhibitory effect on the STNR, and that as the STNR was controlled, many of the children's learning difficulties also started to disappear.

O'Dell and Cook set out to implement Bender's methods at the Bender Institute. They found that not only did learning difficulties improve as the STNR was inhibited, but that signs and symptoms of Attention Deficit Disorder (ADD) and Attention Deficit Hyperactive Disorder (ADHD) also receded.

One study in Germany found a link between a retained STNR in the older child and problems with control of vertical eye movements,[15] suggesting that a retained STNR not only affects postural and muscular capabilities but, like the ATNR and TLR, it is also linked to the development of mature eye movements.

The STNR is one of the first reflexes to re-emerge in old age when joints become stiff and muscle adaptation is less flexible, which can have an effect upon balance. The STNR can be seen returning in the stooped posture and shuffling gait of the old man as he walks along the street. Hand-eye coordination deteriorates, and there is a tendency to become clumsy, dropping things more often. Shakespeare's character Jacques described this cycle as it passes from infancy to old age in, 'The Seven Ages of Man', beginning with:

'At first the infant,
mewling and puking in the nurse's arms...';

and finishing with:

'The sixth stage shifts
Into the lean and slipper'd pantaloon,
With spectacles on nose and pouch on side
His youthful hose well sav'd a world too wide
For his shrunk shank; and his big manly voice,
Turning again towards childish treble, pipes
And whistles in his sound. Last scene of all,
That ends this strange eventful history,
Is second childishness, and mere oblivion,
Sans teeth, sans eyes, sans taste, sans everything.'

Effects of a Retained Symmetrical Tonic Neck Reflex

- Poor upper and lower body integration;
- Posture, particularly when sitting or standing;
- Hypotonia (predominance of floppy muscle tone);
- Poor hand-eye coordination when movements toward and away from the self are required, such as catching a ball and eating;
- Movements that involved upper/lower body coordination such as swimming, forward rolls (somersaults) etc.;
- Judging speed and timing of fast-approaching objects;
- Copying;
- Vertical tracking.

The Rooting and Sucking Reflexes

During uterine development, different parts of the cortex develop at different times. The first region to develop in the human foetus is the part that will represent the mouth and tongue in the motor and somatosensory areas of the brain. The cortex then goes on to develop in concentric zones outward from this core region.

The mouth is the first practice ground for sensory and motor experience, and continues to be one of the most sensitive regions of the body for the remainder of life. It has been suggested that even the simple act of thumb-sucking in the womb helps to stimulate the formation of cortical 'maps' of the mouth and hand,[16] which play a crucial role after birth in the training of skills that require fine muscle coordination such as feeding, speech, and even writing

The rooting reflex emerges between 24 and 28 weeks in utero. After birth, touch on either side of the mouth will elicit turning of the head and opening of the mouth as if searching or 'rooting' for the breast. This rooting response then leads on to sucking movements. The suck reflex can also be directly elicited by touching the nasal fold just above the upper lip.

Peiper observed that after birth, the rooting reaction is an example of early goal-directed behaviour. Initially it is touch alone that results in the turning of the head toward the stimulus, which is usually also the source of food. After a short period of time, a conditioned response will replace the rooting reflex so that *sight* of the breast or bottle will be sufficient to stimulate sucking movements. In other words, vision gradually replaces touch as the stimulus to feeding.

Strength of the rooting reflex is related to hunger and satiety. A hungry baby will root at almost anything rather like a kitten rubbing up against your legs when it is hungry, but it can be difficult to elicit the rooting reflex in a baby who has just been fed.

Michel Odent points out that the rooting reflex is at its most receptive in the first hours after birth, and that the earlier the baby is put to the breast, the more likely it is that breast feeding will be successful. He describes how babies who have to be placed in special care immediately after birth can often be seen rooting in the first few hours after birth, but if for one reason or another they cannot be fed through the usual channel, the rooting reflex will decline in strength over the next few days. It can then be more difficult to activate it at a later stage when the baby is ready to start normal feeding because it was not utilized at its time of optimum 'readiness'.

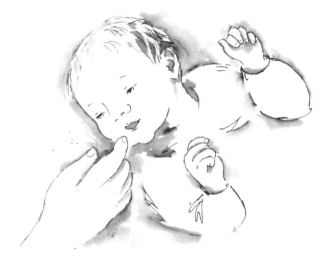

Figure 24. The Rooting Reflex

Figure 25. The Sucking Relex

Sucking is essentially a 'grasp' response. When the child has grown up, it will feed itself by using its hands. At birth, it lacks the coordination to do this, but it is equipped with a group of 'grasp' reflexes. As soon as the mouth comes into contact with the nipple, the baby knows what to do. Earlier maturation of the muscles of the tongue and swallow apparatus compared to other muscle groups means that the mouth can grasp the breast. The tongue presses the nipple up against the palate, which is flatter than the adult palate and is covered with a series of ridges that help to keep the nipple in place.

Sucking and swallowing movements help to develop not only the muscles of the lips and tongue, but also the pharynx, the larynx, and breathing through the nose, all of which will be employed in vocalization and speech some months later. Some observers[17] have noted a relationship between sucking movements and blinking activity, particularly in premature infants, suggesting that there is a connection between mouth movements and eye movements at this early stage in development. (This may be important if the sucking reflex remains present in an older child when the functional link between sucking and blinking movements can impair the autonomy of eye movements such as 'tracking' movements, which are required for more advanced skills such as reading.) Turning of the head, which is part of the rooting response, may also play a part in the development of certain gestural expressions such as nodding and opening of the mouth, which probably lead into the earliest facial movements involved in smiling.[18]

Even after the rooting reflex starts to wane at about 3-4 months of age, the mouth will remain a major source of information. Remember that areas of the cortex involved in representation of the mouth develop in advance of others, providing the core from which other sensory representations develop. When the baby can combine reaching, grasping, and bringing an object to the midline, anything and everything will be placed in the mouth. This helps the baby to learn about size and texture as well as taste before other fine muscle skills, particularly those involving the hand, mature sufficiently to take over from the mouth as the main source of exploration. (Note that objects that are small enough to swallow should never be left within the baby's reach.)

Functions of Rooting and Suck Reflexes

- Initiates searching (rooting), suck reflex, and swallowing (suck reflex);
- Ensures early feeding;
- Response to touch that results in above, eventually transfers from tactile to visual response, so that the *sight* of the breast or bottle will stimulate feeding movements;
- May help to develop the muscle groups involved in smiling.

Effect if retained

- Hypersensitivity in the oral region;
- Continued desire for oral stimulation – needs to chew or suck on something;
- Persistent dribbling;
- Tongue remains too far forward in the mouth, resulting in difficulty chewing solid food. Lack of mature swallowing movements may eventually result in increased arching of the palate (cathedral palate) and need for orthodontic intervention later on);
- Speech and articulation.

The Palmar and Plantar Reflexes

These also belong to the group of 'grasp' reflexes. The Palmar reflex emerges at 11 weeks' gestation and should be inhibited at about 2-3 months of life. Anyone who has ever handled a healthy full-term new-born baby will know how strong the Palmar reflex can be. If a finger is placed firmly in the child's hand, the baby will 'grasp' the finger and can actually suspend its own body weight by this reflex in the first days after birth (this should *not* be tried as an experiment!).

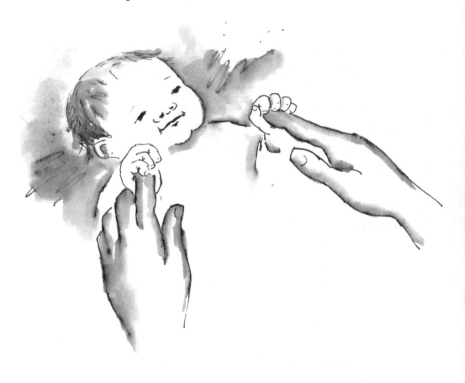

Figure 26. The Palmar Reflex

The Plantar reflex is a similar but weaker response in the feet to pressure being applied to the base of the toes. It appears at about the same time as the Palmar reflex but remains active for slightly longer, until 7-9 months of life.

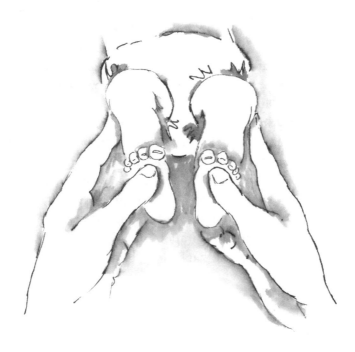

Figure 27. The Plantar Reflex

Both reflexes are thought to be a legacy of an earlier stage in evolution when our ancestors were arborial and the grasping reflexes were necessary to hang on to mother's fur as she moved from place to place. One example can be seen in monkeys at the time of birth. Whereas most human babies are born with the baby's head facing the mother's back, monkeys give birth either on all fours or in a squatting position, and the infant monkey is born facing forward. This means that the mother can reach down to guide the baby in the final stage of birth, and that once the hands are free the infant is strong enough to grab its mother's fur and help to pull itself out. The function of these two reflexes in humans today is less clear, although it is interesting to note that both reflexes grow weaker as the baby's body weight increases.

The Palmar reflex in the hands has a connection to early feeding. When a young mammal sucks at the breast, corresponding kneading movements take place in the hands or front paws. Anyone who has ever bottle-fed a young animal that has lost its mother will have felt these small grasping movements as the infant feeds. The connection works in both directions, and midwives will sometimes use the link to encourage new-born babies to feed. By applying gentle pressure to the palm of the hands or the soles of the feet, a baby who is reluctant to 'latch on' can be encouraged to start sucking. This two-way connection between the hands, and to a lesser degree the soles of the feet and the mouth, is known as the Babkin response and may be important for forging connections between the mouth and the hand in early life, from which other skills will later emerge.

Inhibition of the Palmar reflex is a gradual process that begins with the ability to let go. Parents are usually all too familiar with the stage when their contented child 'drops' a favourite toy. This is followed by protest until the object is retrieved and you are rewarded with wreaths of smiles. Hardly have you turned your back when the toy is dropped again and the period of contentment is mercilessly short-lived. Your baby is actually learning to do something of momentous importance – he is learning how to let go at will. Unless he develops this skill, he will never be able to acquire good manual dexterity, because the Palmar reflex insists that the thumb and all four fingers operate together. This will interfere with fine finger movements, which require each finger to move independently. Letting go is the first stage toward developing a 'pincer' grip a few weeks later. The ability to pick up an object using the thumb and forefinger is one of the most distinctive features of humankind. Not only does it allow manipulation of objects but it also represents the achievement of a major stage of myelination of the cortico-spinal tract (the pathway that runs directly from the motor cortex to the body) and a part of the cerebellum, sometimes know as the 'little brain', which is involved in articulation of the hands and mouth – the latter is essential for speech development.

Children who have undergone neurological assessment at the Institute for Neuro-Physiological Psychology in Chester, who have had a history of speech difficulties but no hearing problems, have all demonstrated difficulty with thumb and finger opposition, coupled with hypersensitivity to gentle stimulation to the palm of the hand. Many also manifest difficulty in separating hand and mouth movements. The continued connection between hand and mouth movements can often be observed in excess hand movements when speaking, and a tendency to move the mouth when engaged in tasks like writing.*

The Plantar reflex in the feet gradually disappears as the feet become involved in locomotion (crawling on the stomach, when the baby will embed the toes into the ground and push forward with the foot), and in weight bearing – i.e. standing and walking. If it persists it can impede crawling, because it is much harder to push forward with a foot when the toes are curled, and it can affect control of upright balance, because the foot cannot provide a secure flexible base for placing and distributing weight.

---

* Schrager[19] also found a connection between difficulty with standing on one leg, and language impairment. Both control of balance *and* rapid alternate movement of the fingers come under the control of different parts of the cerebellum as well as connections to the vestibular system and the motor cortex, giving further weight to the theory that the cerebellar loop is implicated in various language disorders (Levinson, 1984; Nicolson et al., 1994). See Chapter 8.

Functions

- One of the group of 'grasp' reflexes that emerges in utero, starting with the Moro reflex;
- Connected to early feeding via the Babkin response;
- Has an inhibitory effect upon the Moro reflex if the Palmar reflex is elicited immediately *before* activating the Moro reflex.

Effects if retained

- Thumb and finger opposition difficulty;
- Dysdiadochokinesis (rapid alternate movements) of the fingers;
- Writing grip;
- Tactile hypersensitivity;
- Speech and articulation (Babkin response also remains). Tend to 'talk with their hands, write with their mouth';
- *Plantar reflex* – gravitational insecurity resulting from insecure support from the standing base;
- Tendency to 'toe walk'.

Babinski Reflex

The interweaving of one reflex with another can be seen in the relationship between the Plantar and Babinski reflexes during the first year of life. The Babinksi reflex appears at approximately one week of life, and is the opposite of the Plantar response. Pressure applied to the outside edge of the foot results in extension of the great toe and fanning of the other toes. In other words, while the Plantar reflex results in flexion or 'grasping' with the toes, the Babinksi reflex is an extensor reaction.

It remains active for at least the first year of life and may not be completely inhibited until two years of age, when the same stimulus will result in slight flexion of the toes toward the applied pressure.

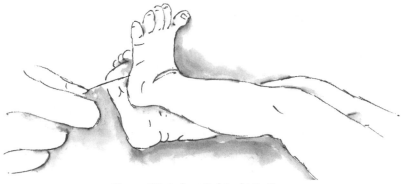

Figure 28. Infant Babinski Reflex

It is thought that the Babinski reflex exerts an inhibitory influence on the Plantar reflex, although both reflexes co-exist for the first 7-9 months of age. Inhibition of the Babinksi reflex occurs with maturation of the corticospinal tract but is released in specific cases of progressive pathology such as multiple sclerosis. (The **Corticospinal tract** is the pathway which runs directly from the motor area of the cortex to the part of the body which it controls.)

Functions

- Thought to play a part in inhibiting the Plantar grasp reflex;
- Should be present when the baby learns to 'commando' crawl, in order to embed the toes into the ground and push with the feet.

Effects if retained

- Indicative of pathology in the upper pyramidal (cortico-spinal) tract. Re-emerges in multiple sclerosis;
- May be temporarily released under conditions of hypoglycaemia, only to disappear within 15 minutes of glucose administration;
- Affects muscles at the back of the legs affecting gait.

The Spinal Galant Reflex

In 1917, Galant gave his name to a reflex, which emerges at 20 weeks' gestation. Stimulation of the skin on either side of the spine in the lumbar region causes flexion of the hip on the side that has been stimulated and arching of the remainder of the body in the opposite direction in an avoidance reaction.

Figure 29 The Spinal Galant Reflex

It is thought that, like the ATNR, the Spinal Galant reflex helps to facilitate movement of the foetus inside the womb and assists in the birth process. In a mother who is fairly slim, the Galant movement can sometimes be seen as a squirming or fish-like movement of the baby in the later stages of pregnancy when it changes position. During a normal delivery, the vaginal wall exerts pressure on the lumbar region during each contraction. This pressure activates the Spinal Galant reflex, lending flexibility to the hips and helping the baby to 'turn' as it negotiates its way down the birth canal.

Other functions of the Spinal Galant reflex are more speculative, but it has been suggested that it might act as a primitive conductor of sound in utero,[20] helping vibrations to pass down the spinal column so that they are 'felt' through bone conduction. Another suggestion is that it is a reminder of the tail we once shared with our ancestors and had for a short time during our early embryonic period. Phylogenetically, it originated as a skin reflex of the spine at the reptilian and amphibian stages of evolution, and is seen in swimming creatures and creatures that move on all fours. Once the upright posture is achieved, locus of postural control moves to the front of the body and the continued presence of a Spinal Galant reflex becomes a hindrance to postural stability and upright locomotion. In the normal developing infant, it should be inhibited by nine months of age.

If it remains active for a prolonged period, it is associated with hypersensitivity of the lumbar region. The reflex can be activated by even the lightest touch and is sometimes a feature in children who dislike clothing with a tight waistband, belts, certain fabrics, etc. It is sometimes found in children who continue to wet the bed above the age of 5, although it is by no means a universal factor. It can cause difficulties in sitting still and paying attention, and if present strongly on one side only can contribute to the development of scoliosis (curvature) of the spine.

In common with other reflexes, inhibition is a gradual process over the course of the first nine months of life, which should take place as more complex reflexes, postural control, and movement capabilities develop. Plenty of opportunity for stimulation of the lumbar region, together with free movement of the legs when lying on the back, seem to be two environmental factors that play a significant part in helping the reflex to come under increasing cortical control. Once again, the floor provides an ideal playground from where these movements can be practised.

Functions of the Spinal Galant Reflex

- Hip flexibility that may assist in the birth process as a result of pressure on the lumbar region;
- May act as a primitive conductor of sound (bone conduction up and down the spinal column) in utero;
- May help to inhibit the ATNR and bring in the Amphibian reflex;
- Appears to be connected to urinary and intestinal functioning.

Effects if retained

- Fidget/need to be on the move all the time;
- Sitting still/concentration/ short-term memory problems;
- Bedwetting;
- Exaggerated hip rotation to one side when walking;
- (Sometimes present in children who continue to soil – Asperger's syndrome).

The reflexes mentioned above are only a selection of *some* of the reflexes that play a part in the early development of motor and related skills. As these early reflexes are practised, transformed, and integrated into the service of higher skills, as the child passes through the various motor milestones such as learning how to sit, roll over, crawl on the tummy, creep on hands knees, develop a pincer grip, and eventually to stand and walk. This is only the *beginning* of balance and coordination, but it provides the foundation from where all other skills become possible.

Postural reflexes, sometimes also known as righting and equilibrium reactions, then gradually take over the functions of some of the primitive reflexes over the course of the first $3^1/_2$ years of life.[21] These later reflexes help to give fluidity to movement, a sound basis for balance, and improved adaptability to alterations in the environment.

Movement capabilities also reflect efficiency of functioning within the brain, both in a hierarchical sense and in communication between the two hemispheres of the cerebral cortex. There is increasing evidence to suggest that under-developed postural reflexes can, at a later stage in life, have an effect on advanced learning and social adaptability,[22] both of which require flexibility of thinking and response. This is hardly surprising when we remember that reflex movement in nerve cells lies at the root of every act of higher will; the highest acts of will merely have deliberation, choice, and inhibition added to these foundation reflexes.[23] If reflexes themselves have failed to adapt with maturity, other adaptive functions will also be affected.

The majority of children pass through these stages of development with ease, naturally playing out their evolutionary heritage and achieving bipedalism with the important building blocks in place. Nature and nurture work together to provide the raw material and the environment with which important motor milestones can be reached. If, for any reason, a child does not pass through these stages spontaneously, then an understanding of the processes involved can be useful in helping parents and professionals to provide a suitable environment in which to bridge the gaps.

5. The Music of Language

> 'Music is a matter of the heart.'
>
> Pahlen
>
> 'The heart knows reasons which reason itself cannot understand.'
>
> Blaise Pascal

When my second son was about 18 months old, he was diagnosed as having a hearing impairment. All the usual investigations and surgical interventions were carried out but still his hearing seemed to hover at 60 decibels. We were told that he had remarkably small ear canals – too small to insert either grommets or a hearing aid – and that one canal would have to be surgically widened in order to fit a hearing aid at a later date. This was done, and at two years of age he was given a hearing aid, and a teacher for the deaf started to visit us at home to teach us the rudiments of sign language. We were told that he would probably have some speech and language problems, and because reading, writing, and spelling are linked to speech, we should expect that he might have some specific learning difficulties at a later age. We were also told 'to remain friendly with an ear, nose, and throat surgeon for many years to come'.

When he was three, we moved house and the process of

assessment started all over again. The good news was that the hearing impairment was not as severe as first feared and he could probably 'get by' without using a hearing aid. The bad news was that this meant that neither he nor we were entitled to continued support from the services for the deaf.

William's speech and language progressed and he started school. Whilst he would talk to us and his brother and sister at home, after half a term we were told that no one had heard him speak at school. Apparently he did have friends in the playground, he was cooperative, and he would willingly get on with his work, but he did not talk. By six and a half years of age the situation had not changed, and he was showing no sign of learning to read. In all other respects he was just like any other child and there were no obvious speech or language problems at home. The situation gradually improved with a change of school at 7; reading started to catch up, he started to talk away from home, and he made a good friend. We allowed matters to continue as they were until, a couple of years later, his older brother was admitted as a chorister to the cathedral choir in Chester.

Since the demise of many cathedral schools, recruitment of boys and families who are prepared to devote the time to having a chorister in the family can be a problem (despite the unparalleled opportunities such an education provides). The Master of Choristers suggested that while one boy was in the choir, we might like to audition the other one! During his introductory talk to parents, he also mentioned that, 'all my boys' reading age improves by 12 months within 6 months of joining the choir, irrespective of whether they were good or poor readers at the time of joining'.[24]

William did eventually join his brother some 18 months later. We decided that if he passed an audition on his own merit without anyone knowing of his hearing problem, he would probably cope with the demands of being a chorister. He had one advantage in that he came from a musical family where he had been surrounded by the sounds of classical music from the moment of conception.

Three years later, William was head chorister. He entered secondary school without any specific learning difficulties and at the end of his school career he was made Head Boy. He also passed his performer's certificate as a Bass Baritone at the age of 17, and went on to university, where he was offered a choral scholarship at the end of his first year. No one is aware that he still has a 40-60 decibel hearing loss in certain frequencies. The years when he made the greatest progress were the years when he started to sing. William's story, together with the Master of Choristers' comment about reading, led me to ask – 'Why?....'. Why *does* music, and singing in particular, have such a significant impact on other language skills?

The story of music takes us back to the world of movement and to an almost universal medium of communication – dance. Dance is the expression of emotion through movement, and in primitive peoples, dance rituals begin with rhythm – the beating of feet, the clapping of hands, the beating of a drum. Dance can exist without music simply as movement in time and space – this is the beginning of rhythm.

Both rhythm and sound are created as a result of movement – rhythm is a sequence of movements in time, and sound is made up of vibrations. Dr Alfred Tomatis, an ear, nose, and throat surgeon in France who developed a system of sound therapy for treating a range of disorders – from opera singers who had lost the ability to pitch certain notes, to children with language impairments – observed that both rhythm and sound are processed through different parts of the human ear. He described the vestibular apparatus as being 'the ear of the body', the part that is involved in the feeling and production of movement and rhythm, while the cochlea or hearing apparatus deals with the perception of sounds or pitch.

Through the vestibular system, rhythm becomes a body-based function. Where there is movement there is frequency, and whenever there is frequency there is sound, so that sound is a product of anything that moves. Both chambers within the inner ear need to work together to produce the dual elements of music – rhythm and sound.

Other senses are also involved in musical experience. Sound is a sensation transmitted to the brain as an electrical signal that has been caused by vibrations that have passed through the ear. Vibration is carried to the ear through various media such as air, water, wood, or the skull. The ear detects vibrations that travel in the form of sound waves of varying frequency. The human ear has the potential to detect frequencies from 16 hz (low sounds) up to 25000 hz (high sounds). The frequency determines not only the pitch but also, to some extent, which of the sensory systems will pick up the vibration. For example, low frequency sounds (below 100 hz) are often 'felt' as vibrations through the skin rather than 'heard'. These low frequency vibrations cause the hairs on the dermis of the skin to stand up, and different parts of the body may sense the vibration dissonance. Slow movement and rhythm are detected by the vestibular system and the body – indeed, it is difficult *not* to move in time to certain rhythms. Modern rock music, which is based largely on low frequency sound and 'beat', makes us want to move. It stimulates the body to mimic the movements of the music and, as Paul Madaule says, 'makes us want to gyrate and hardly moves above the belt'. Higher frequencies enter the hearing domain.

Classical music, on the other hand, contains a wider spectrum of frequencies and is far richer in the high frequencies. Tomatis described high frequency sound as 'energizing', stimulating arousal in those higher regions of the brain that are associated with attention, whilst low-frequency sound tends to be enervating and must be played at a much greater volume to have the same impact. In different moods or stages of life we may seek out particular types of music to enhance or dampen the feelings and needs of the moment.

Both the sound and the rhythmic elements of music have the power to communicate. In this sense, music is another form of language, and if *movement* is a child's first language, music is the second.

Before a child can speak (and the word 'infant' means 'one without speech'), the cooing of the young baby has pitch, intonation, and cadence. Babbling is a form of tone and staccato rhythm, both of which are key elements of music and language. Babies will imitate the timbre and cadences of adult speech before they learn to talk, as if they are practising the melody of a song for which they do not yet have the words. This is the vocal equivalent of building a library of sounds from which a vocabulary of language will be constructed. Voice and ear must work as cooperative partners in this process.

The human foetus can hear from about six months after conception, although external sounds are muffled through the barrier of the mother's abdominal wall. The inside of the womb is probably a very noisy place – the internal workings of the mother's digestive tract and other systems provide acoustic stimulation from the moment of conception, as does the continuous accompaniment of her heartbeat. The sounds that the foetus hears are quite different from the sounds that we are used to, because the foetus is surrounded by fluid and absorbent tissue, which prevent the *higher* frequencies being transmitted. Only low-to-medium frequencies covering the range from 40-4000 hz will be heard by the developing baby, sounds which coincidentally correspond to the range of notes on the piano and the range contained within most vocal melodies. The rhythm, timbre, and cadence of his mother's speech, however, will be the same from intra-uterine to extra-uterine existence and will already be familiar by the time of birth.

Tomatis suggests that the sound of the mother's voice provides an acoustic link from life in the womb to the development of speech and language. Our own voice carries within it the melodies and patterns of our parents' speech. When my father first heard a recording of my eldest son singing as a treble, he thought that it was me as a child. The same son is now a true bass who sings with the voice of his father, but within that voice is contained the colour and the brightness of the unbroken voice.

Whilst in the womb, the foetus has been in contact with the elements of both music and spoken language – rhythm (the arrangement of a collection of sounds in time), beat (a regular metred pattern), pulse (the rate or pace of music), and the overriding melody of his mother's voice. Pulse is slightly different from both rhythm and beat; whereas rhythm describes the arrangement or pattern of sounds in time (phrases – phrasing develops naturally from the breathing rhythm of speech), beat is a regular metred pattern. Pulse in music (just like the human pulse rate) can vary, speeding up or slowing down to give expressive quality to the sounds being played. We do the same in speech, emphasizing some words, pausing over others, and hurrying over the connecting words that lead us to the point we wish to make.

In the first few days after birth, the new-born's ears are partially filled with fluid. Until this fluid clears, the baby inhabits an auditory hinterland between the uterine and extra-uterine world. Once the fluid has cleared, the baby's ears open up to a wide frequency of sounds – something in the region of 16-20,000 hz – sounds which we as adults have gradually lost the ability to 'hear'. From the moment of birth we begin to become progressively deaf, because we need to learn to listen *selectively* in order to speak. In other words, we need to narrow down the focus of our listening to a smaller specific range of frequencies; the frequencies of our own language.

Most languages fall within the range of 125-8,000 hz. In the first few years of life, a baby must learn to 'fine tune' its hearing so that it is most sensitive and discriminative within this relatively narrow band. Furthermore, every language has its own frequency curve; that is, a collection of specific sounds that are unique to each language and which require different levels of sensitivity at different frequencies in order to be able to hear, understand, and reproduce those sounds through the vocal tract. In other words, the developing child must learn to 'tune in' to the sounds of its mother tongue as if it was selecting a radio station. In the first three years of life, a child has the potential to learn any language on earth if it is exposed to the sounds of that language regularly over a long enough period of time. After three years of age, the window of opportunity starts to close, and by six years of age the capacity to learn language as an innate skill starts to diminish.

Hearing also has a spatial aspect. A new-born baby reacts to sound rather like an animal in the wild, by 'freezing' momentarily when touched by strange or unfamiliar sounds. This moment of 'freeze' suspends response while the young creature waits to find out whether the sound heralds comfort or danger. In the young baby, the eyes will also respond to unfamiliar sounds by opening in a startle reaction and then darting from place to place in an attempt to locate the source of sound. When the eyes eventually alight upon the stimulus, the first stage in visual fixation to the source of sound, or *orientation*, has occurred. In this way hearing (orientation to sound) helps to support balance (internal compass) and vision in locating not only our own position in space but also awareness of position of factors outside of the self.

The higher frequencies are particularly important because

they signify space and direction to the infant, rather like laser beams. They are absorbed by soft surfaces but reflect off hard surfaces, revealing the presence of acoustic 'shadows' or objects cast in their path. The new-born, with its greater sensitivity to high frequency sounds, hears echoes and reverberations, so that if a door is banged the sound will be echoed back many times. As adults, we can experience this in buildings that have been designed to be acoustically 'alive' – cathedrals, tunnels, and old-fashioned school halls that have wooden floors. How many of us as children played with the echo of our own voice, fascinated by its ability to return to us? This echo effect is the beginning of focused listening.

Orientation to sound is also possible because we have two ears, and the distance from either ear to the source of sound is different. Over time, the brain learns to compare the time it takes for a sound to reach each ear and locate the source of sound by using the small time difference to detect *where* the sound is coming from. If there is hearing loss in either ear, it can prevent the brain from being able to compute these minute time differences accurately. Vision tells us what is happening in front and to the sides; hearing and balance help us to know what is happening behind. If you have ever walked down a busy street with someone who has become hard of hearing, they often appear to be very rude because they are blissfully unaware of anyone behind them who may be trying to get past. This is because they no longer have the extra sense to inform them of what is happening beyond their field of vision.

The ability to match sounds and sights together will take many years to develop, and is essential for both reading and writing later on. Reading requires the translation of visual symbols on a page into an internal auditory image that we can 'hear' inside our head as if we were reading aloud. Writing involves the opposite process; the translation of an auditory image (idea) inside the head into an appropriate visual symbol on the page.[25] Thus, the matching of visual to auditory stimuli and vice versa are important for many higher aspects of learning.

The matching process also involves the motor system. The eye movements necessary visually to locate the source are a motor ability, and speech (the vocal expression of innate language) cannot occur without control of the muscles at the front of the mouth, the tongue, the swallow mechanism, and breathing. The process of 'giving voice' to sounds helps to integrate the working of the hearing and motor systems.

Whereas hearing is used to locate sounds that come from outside, the voice occupies an *inner* space inside the head. Voice frequencies should go to both ears, having a centralizing function, so that the voice comes from the centre of the self. In this sense, voice is outwardly directed but self-orienting, whereas hearing is inwardly directed and outwardly oriented.

Use of the voice in play, speech, chant, and song can help to develop orientation, attention, sound discrimination, and memory. Through music, the senses are refined and the musical and rhythmic aspects of language can be developed to assist higher cognitive learning. Music helps to join brain and body in their response to the resonance of sound so that the body itself becomes an instrument of expression.

Different parts of the body resonate to different frequencies of sound. When sounds 'hit' those resonance points it can have a profound effect upon the individual. We are all familiar with the 'tingle' factor, when a certain piece of music causes hairs on the back of the neck or the spine to stand on end, or when a particular passage, chord, or sequence in music reaches down into the pit of the stomach. In theory, every region of the body can act as a resonator; when a sound from outside matches the frequencies of the body, we feel as if we are 'at one' with the music itself.

Professional musicians seem to develop a particular capacity to strike the resonance points of others – this is when music really 'sings' to us. Singers, for example, do not simply produce sounds from the vocal chords: sound is amplified as a result of resonance cavities within the body that can be loosely defined as the nose, mouth, neck, and chest. These resonance points are the localities in which the physical sensations (vibrations) are felt when the voice is used, and they are responsible for the tone or ring of the voice. According to Tomatis, 'the voice can only produce what the ear can hear', but the ear's powers of discrimination are improved through using the voice. Voicing helps to improve listening, memory, and articulation.

Not only does every language comprise a different range of frequencies, but also, articulation of different languages involves a slightly different part of the speech apparatus. I remember a French woman saying to me a number of years ago, in response to one of my truly appalling attempts at speaking French, 'Oh, you English, you are so lazy. No wonder you cannot speak French; you never use your *lips*.' It is true that to speak French without an accent, the English need to move the locus of speech further forward in the mouth to make greater use of the lips and the nasal cavities; and we also have to change the point of emphasis within the word. Just as in learning to read and spell their first language, children need the opportunity to 'feel' the sounds in the mouth, when learning a new language, as adults we also need time to 'practise' the sounds of speech.

Alteration of the part of the mouth also has an effect upon the tone of voice. If you listen very carefully, this linguistic 'tone' can even be heard in the singing of different nationalities.

The traditional sound of trebles in an English Cathedral choir is a 'pure' sound – the high notes sound like the ring of fine glass crystal; the lower notes are more like the piping of a wooden flute. The boys of the Vienna Boys' Choir make a much fuller, fruitier sound that at times is almost womanly. Les Petits Chanteurs à la Croix de Bois in Paris produce a reedier timbre – all are characteristic of the part of the mouth from where the sounds of speech are regularly produced. Thus, even in music, the dialect of the region can be heard.

Feedback from the voice to the ears helps to improve auditory discrimination, and as the ear become more 'attuned', tone of voice, accuracy of pitch, and inflection are refined. I have no doubt that the years William spent singing helped to complete the break in the audio-vocal feedback loop, which had occurred as a result of early hearing impairment. As the voice was able to make up the sounds, which originally the ear could not hear, so the associated problems started to remit.

6. Music and the Brain

'The wood of a Cremona violin only played by the hands of a master will develop a molecular tendency to harmonise resonance.'

Halleck, 1898

Music and language have many elements in common. Both are expressions of the organization of sound in time and space. Music is language without words. In common with other languages, it imposes order, structure, timing, rhythm, and sound frequency discrimination on random sound. In effect, it gives meaning to sound.

In terms of both evolution and development it can be understood at the most primitive levels, for music is processed at all levels in the brain. From the brain stem it can affect heart rate, breathing, and arousal; through the limbic system it has a powerful impact upon feelings and emotions; in the cortex it can create visual images and associations – and it is in the cortex that it is understood at an intellectual level. In this respect, music has the power to affect all levels of the human psyche.

Music is one of life's earliest natural teachers. Before birth, the foetus reacts to music with changes in motor activity, and infants respond to music and can imitate simple rhythms before they develop speech. The early cooing of the baby has both melody and intonation. In the absence of musical training, music is perceived primarily in the right hemisphere of the brain, the side of the brain responsible for melody recognition, language *comprehension*, rhythm, spatial orientation, and picture recognition.

These are abilities that are used in the early years of teaching a child to read, particularly with the whole-word, look-say method. Nursery rhymes, songs, and movement to music can all be used in the first five years to develop other skills in preparation for literacy. Musical training also helps to develop left-hemisphere abilities such as sound discrimination, timing, numeric skills, and expressive language. These abilities are essential for the understanding of phonics, and for developing short-term memory in the absence of visual cues.

Singing and instrumental training develop fine muscle coordination, but they also train the matching of motor output to visual input. Sequencing ability is developed, for a melody and musical phrases naturally contain a beginning, middle, and end, which follow one upon another until a cadence is reached – a natural form of grammar. One study from the University of London[26] found that successful tonal memory and chord analysis accuracy bore a clear relationship to reading age, independent of chronological age or IQ. Children who did best musically showed the highest reading ages. The researchers surmised that the storing of sound sequences and analysis of complex sounds for components are akin to aspects of reading.

This was illustrated by a small experiment carried out by a teacher with a reception class in a school in South Wales.[27] The teacher asked a colleague who was a music teacher to compose a series of 3-4 note tunes, using notes that approximately corresponded in frequency to sounds of the alphabet. The children began by listening to the tunes for a few minutes each day. They then started to hum or sing along to the tunes, and a little later they put specific letter sounds to the tunes. At the end of the school year, none of the children in the class had any problems with learning to read.

A similar experiment was carried out in Denmark, where a small group of reception class children were given daily sessions using song and dance with no formal tuition in reading. At the end of three months, the phonological awareness of this group was found to be ahead of a control group who had received specific teaching in phonological awareness.

Dr Kjeld Johansen, also working in Denmark, has used a series of frequency-specific music tapes to improve the hearing discrimination and speed of processing of more than a thousand children diagnosed with dyslexia. At the end of one year there was a 70 per cent remission in signs of dyslexia in the group. Other studies carried out by Rauscher and Shaw (1996) at the University of California demonstrated a clear causal link between music and spatial intelligence. They showed that the spatial reasoning performance of 19 pre-school children who received eight months of music lessons far exceeded the spatial reasoning performance of a demographically comparable group of 15 pre-school children who did not have music lessons. Spatial intelligence is the ability to perceive the visual world accurately, to form mental images of physical objects, and to recognize variations of objects.

Scientists at the Chinese University of Hong Kong[28] have found that children who played musical instruments had significantly better verbal memory than others. In a study of 90 boys aged 6-15, half had musical training and played in the school orchestra for between one and five years, while the other half did not have any regular musical training. Tests for verbal memory were carried out on both groups, and students with musical training showed significantly better word recall than those without. A follow-up study a year later found that children who had stopped playing an instrument had retained the level of verbal memory they had whilst still playing, but could not keep up with those who continued to play on a regular basis. The scientist who led the experiment, Dr Agnes Chan, likened the effect to the way that runners find that stronger legs help them to play a better standard of tennis.

Playing a musical instrument or singing involves the training of motor skills as well as sound, rhythm, and pattern recognition. The matching of motor output to sounds and visual symbols is fundamental to reading and writing. It is highly probable that the more adept a child becomes at recognizing and reproducing sounds through the motor system, the better related functions become. This may be particularly important in the light of various studies that have examined the effect of phonological training on children with dyslexia. Whilst the training of phonological awareness using language sounds seems to help, in many cases it has not resolved all of the literacy problems associated with dyslexia. One reason for this may be that additional time is not given to the training of motor skills – something which is an intrinsic part of any form of musical training.

The Power of Singing

Singing is particularly powerful in entraining the listening and voicing skills which underlie spoken and written language. Paula Tallal at Rutgers University in New Jersey demonstrated that certain children diagnosed with dyslexia are slower at decoding the sounds of speech and do not 'hear' some of the smaller sounds within individual words. A word such as 'remember' may be spelled 'rember' if the child has failed to perceive the full length of the word and the vowel sounds that lie between the consonants. Interestingly, young children often make this sort of mistake in the initial stages of learning to read and write, writing 'cat' as 'ct' and 'Mummy' as 'Mmy'. Tallal has developed a computer program that slows down the sounds of speech to allow the child extra time to hear every sound within a word. Singing or chanting also has the effect of slowing down the sounds of speech.

Most vocal music has its origins in religious rites when music was learned by heart through repetition, and chants were a stylized form of speech in which every syllable was intoned on a single tone of comfortable pitch. The principle of giving a tonal and time value to each syllable persists in song and chant today. For example, a simple sentence such as,

'Lord, now lettest thou thy servant depart in peace'

is quite different when set to music:

'Lor--d, n ow lett-est thou thy ser-vant depar-t in pea--ce.'

Vowel sounds are given extended time value in singing. The consonants stop and start sound, giving sound structure (and meaning) to the words. The setting of words to music gives the singer and listener more time in which to hear and process all of the sounds within each word, particularly the vowel sounds which provide colour and contour, and which are necessary for reading and spelling.

Singing is often done from memory and practised by repetition. Short-term memory is enhanced as a result of repetition. A chorister may spend 20 hours a week singing. While he is singing, he is also listening, vocalizing, scanning, and memorizing reading material, much of which is far in advance of his actual reading level. He may also sing in other languages such as Latin and modern languages that he has not come across at school. He does not necessarily understand the content of what he is singing, but the 'ear' for the sounds of each language is being trained.

Choristers serve a probationary period during which they learn their trade. In common with other apprenticeships, the probationer learns from the senior choristers beside him. To begin with s/he may only mouth the words in fear of making a mistake, but the more s/he listens, and the more s/he sings, the better his or her own performance becomes.

Sound and Voice

The process of 'sounding out' or voicing aloud is important for developing an 'inner ear' for the sounds of speech and written language. This 'inner ear' helps us to 'hear' sounds, ideas, and thoughts inside our head, as if we were speaking aloud. Children go through a developmental stage when they spend much of their playtime engaged in private speech, creating imaginary conversations between their toys. I remember an occasion when one of my children was sent to her room for some misdemeanour. I went upstairs about 15 minutes later to tell her that she could come down, only to find that she had laid her dolls out in a row and was happily imitating me, telling her off. Her dolls were answering back, and she was so absorbed by her newly found authority that she was not bothered about coming downstairs to join the rest of the family.

This period of giving voice to thoughts and feelings is an important stage in identifying or finding language with which to express them. As the system matures, such thoughts become internalized and we learn to select when to say what is in our mind and when to keep quiet.

Learning to read involves a similar process. Children need plenty of opportunity to read out loud before they can internalize the sounds of speech and read fluently to themselves. Written language is the product of an oral culture in which stories and knowledge was passed down from one generation to the next through the spoken word. It is only   relatively recently that the majority of the population has become literate and we have become a predominantly visual culture. But in order to read, we still need to pass through the oral stage of sounding out the words to match the sound to the written symbol. Singing, and sounding out as a class help to do just this.

It has been suggested[29] that neurological changes occur when people chant or sing as a group:

'Their central nervous system activity becomes synchronous; they become like, or of, one mind. Their stress hormones decrease, muscle tension decreases and the heart rate normalises. More oxygen enters the system, just by virtue of breathing in and out. You can think of it as controlled hyperventilation and we know that when people hyperventilate they enter into altered states. They feel high, have a certain clarity of mind and sometimes physical vision.'

Sound stimulation is preparation for work on the voice. Vocal experience supports learning by incorporating language into the self. In order to find meaning, what you receive through your senses must also pass through yourself, and this is the *doing* stage that facilitates integration. Paul Madaule[30] from the Listening Centre in Toronto says that 'work on the voice can be a route to self-sufficiency. The sense of self (the answer to the question, who am I?) is strengthened by use of the voice.'

Music and the Brain

Musical *meaning* is achieved without words and tends to create visual images in the mind of the listener – a right-brain function – illustrated by the fact that certain styles of orchestration are actually known as 'mood painting'. The process of 'sounding out' involves the left brain, whilst music helps to build a storehouse of vocabulary (right brain), or reference library of sounds which can be called upon at any time. In other words, music helps to train *both* sides of the brain.

Language also involves both sides of the brain. While the right side is more involved with the non-verbal and emotional aspects of language (body language, intuition, and the meaning behind the words), the verbal aspects of language are predominantly a left-brain function. The articulate brain is the product of earlier stages of motor, sensory, and emotional language. These are all stepping-stones on the road to verbal fluency.

A number of authors have suggested that up until about age 7, the right hemisphere matures slightly ahead of the left. The right hemisphere also has more connections downward to those lower centres in the brain concerned with feelings, emotions, hormones, sensory experience, and survival functions. Alan Schore[31] poses a case for both sides of the brain being involved in a kind of juggling act during development – sometimes one side taking the lead, and sometimes the other. In order to have a command of language, both sides need to have received an adequate period of entrainment. The right side seems to learn from sensory, motor, and emotional experience, while the left is more technical in its specific skills. Both sides need to work together as cooperative partners and to exchange information in either direction with equal efficiency. Interaction between the two sides of the brain is made possible by the corpus callosum – millions and millions of nerve fibres which act like connecting telephone wires to enable instantaneous communication between the two cerebral hemispheres.

Tomatis observed that in cases of dyslexia and stammering, the individual does not seem to have established a preferred ear for processing the sounds of speech. He maintained that the *right* ear is the most efficient for decoding language sounds because signals from the right ear pass directly to the main processing centre of language on the left side of the brain. Sounds heard through the *left* ear are first sent to the right hemisphere, but must then cross over the corpus callosum back to the main language centre on the left side to be decoded. In terms of milliseconds, the route from the left ear takes fractionally longer and may be associated with delay, confusion, or interference when listening or speaking.

A number of systems of sound therapy have been developed which use music to improve auditory processing. One such system, devised by Dr Kjeld Johansen at the Baltic Dyslexia Research Laboratory, uses frequency-specific music tapes to improve sound discrimination and efficiency of processing in children with dyslexia. The children are given a hearing test that measures hearing thresholds from 125-8,000 hz, followed by a dichotic listening test which assesses which ear is the more efficient and preferred for processing language sounds. Many of the children show either a strong left ear preference or have failed to establish a leading ear. Whilst undergoing a course of sound therapy, many of these children become more strongly left-eared for a period of time before settling for right ear dominance. One reason may be that, during the *early* stages of language acquisition, language is actually a right-hemisphere function connected to multi-sensory and emotional events. Only as verbal skills become more sophisticated does the left hemisphere assume overall control over language abilities. This hypothesis is in tune with Schore's theory that both sides of the cortex are trained in different ways at different times before they specialize in particular functions.

Forty years ago, no one thought it odd to learn the alphabet to a tune, days of the week and months of the year to a rhyme, and multiplication tables or Latin verbs to a chant. The education revolution of the 1960s threw some of these ideas out, arguing that children need to learn concepts first – the knowledge of tables, it was said, without understanding the meaning of multiplication did not produce mathematicians later on. Nevertheless, it would appear that children are most receptive to just this type of rote learning between the ages of 4 and 7 – a time when it is generally accepted that the right hemisphere is slightly ahead of the left in development.

Babies respond to the tonal and rhythmic qualities of stories long before they understand the stories themselves. This suggests that the musical elements of language convey meaning before words take shape in the mind. It has sometimes been said that feral children, children who have been brought up in the wild without human contact, have no memory of their experiences before they were 'found' by society. This is highly debatable. What is more probable is that feral children have no language with which to communicate their life experiences prior to coming into contact with civilization because they had no verbal language at that time. They do, however, have a sensory and emotional language, which has been stored as sights, smells, sounds, and feelings. These sensory-emotional experiences become part of somatic memory. The body can have a memory of its own, of which the mind is not even aware.

Babies and young children share a similar sensory-emotional language that is forgotten when spoken language starts to develop. The process of being able to name objects, thoughts, and feelings allows the primal language to retreat into the deeper reaches of the brain as if words operate as a memory wash that results in amnesia for pre-verbal language.

C. S. Lewis illustrated this concept allegorically in the final book of the Chronicles of Narnia, *The Last Battle*. Three of the four children have returned to Narnia for the last time. Narnia is a magical country that can be found only by those who are called to it, or those who stumble by accident through one of the doorways between this world and Narnia. In Narnia, the animals and the trees can talk. One of the elders of Narnia asks the three children where the fourth child, Susan, is. The reply is that Susan is no longer a friend of Narnia. She has entered the adult world, becoming interested in clothes and make-up, and she has lost the ability to understand the language of the animals or to hear the trees. In growing up, we lose part of our childish selves in the pursuit of maturity. If we are lucky, the former child is integrated into the developing adult.

What Else Does Music Do?

Roger Fisher,[32] who for many years was Organist and Master of Choristers at Chester Cathedral, made a distinction between the effects of musical performance as opposed to musical listening. He pointed out some of the additional skills that are needed for performance, which are not recruited in passive listening:

- Singers need to use mental abilities to pitch notes in their minds just ahead of each sound they make (visualization of pitch and anticipatory use of the internal ear).
- Pianists and instrumentalists need to foresee fingering problems and solve them both for technical security and artistic phrasing (motor planning).
- All musical performers need to develop quick reflexes to respond either to a conductor's beat or to the contributions of other performers (motor performance).
- All need to combine the capacity to perform correctly with an ability to communicate musical style and emotion to their listeners (communication through sensitive use of tone, dynamics, phrasing, and timing).

This combination of skills once again involves the translation and integration of sensory to *motor* skills with continuous feedback from the motor system back to the ear and the eye.

Music and Number

As early as the sixth century, Anicius Boethius described music as being 'number made audible'.

> 'To medieval thinkers, arithmetic, the science of number, was fundamental. Music was the expression of number in time, giving pitch, duration, rhythm, stress and accent to the words. Language, regulated by number was song. Number structuring space was geometry. Number in time and space gave rise to the cosmic dance or the harmony of the spheres: astronomy – like the Pythagoreans before them, the Fathers of the Church and the Schoolmen perceived the universe as essentially musical.'[33]

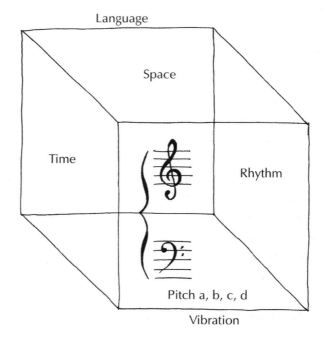

Figure 30. The Three Dimensions of Music

Arousal, Attention, and Creativity

Neurological arousal depends on the interplay between repetition and novelty. Too much novelty results in over-arousal, poorly sustained attention, and heightened anxiety. Paucity of novelty and a surfeit of repetition result in boredom, fatigue and 'shutting off'. Composers and performers alike learn to manipulate sound, rhythm, and dynamics to create an every-changing balance between these dual elements. 'The key feature of the best music of any period is the well-balanced diet of heightened emotional tension, followed by periods of relaxation and rest.'[34]

States of arousal are accompanied by beta electrical activity in the brain (see Table 1). The characteristic of beta activity is that it is fast frequency, randomized, and not very synchronous. This means that the pattern of activity within the brain tends to be asymmetrical, with certain areas being very active and other areas at rest. The next level down from beta is alpha – alpha activity is more regular, rhythmic, tranquil, and organized. Slow classical music is associated with more alpha brain-wave activity. In other words, when listening to classical music, there is a tendency for brain wave activity to slow down and become more synchronous – a state revered in Eastern cultures where the aim is to slow down the brainwaves in order to hear a higher mind.[35] 'Alpha states' are associated with a relaxed waking state, when thoughts 'free wheel', new ideas surface, and from where a solution to an old problem gradually floats up to consciousness. More synchronous states may be associated with improved communication between the left and right hemispheres in both directions, hence the ability to solve problems when relaxed, which seem insoluble when under stress. If brain waves are moving together rather than independently, in the absence of epileptic seizure, it is assumed that those areas are coordinating their activity – one of the highest levels of brain-wave coherence ever observed has been from musicians mentally rehearsing their compositions.

Table 1[36]
Human Brain Waves and Associated States of Arousal

Type	Frequency	Associated State
Delta	0.5-3 hz	Drowsy
Theta	4-7 hz	Meditative states, unconscious processing: information processing in the hippocampus and Rapid Eye Movement (REM) sleep
Alpha	8-12 hz	Relaxed waking state
Beta	13-30 hz	Cognitive and emotional activation, shifting of attention to specific stimulus/task

---

Certain combinations of rhythm and pulse can also cause a shift in brain-wave state as well as altering the body's own internal rhythms. For example, the strict 2/4 rhythm of marching time has an emboldening effect, while syncopation (emphasis on the 'off' beat) creates a feeling of excited anticipation. Slow movements from the Baroque period mimic the heartbeat, thereby altering the mood to one of quiet contemplation. Melody with stepwise upward phrasing creates tension, while stepwise downward movement of the melody causes relaxation and completion. Other musical devices such as modulating from major to minor key, use of dissonance and resolution in harmony, and the use of sequences can have a similar effect in shifting arousal and consciousness and producing states of tension and relaxation. The process of attention results from a state of tension induced by the arousal of appropriate nerve cells similar to the tension of an Aeolian harp vibrating in the wind with sufficient intensity to produce sound.

Nature finds expression through music – from the whispering of the wind in the leaves to the thundering of a stormy sea on the shore. Just as all living things share the characteristic of motion, all of life is sound, 'because sound is the product of anything that moves'.[37] The enjoyment of music, whether it is dance (moving to sound) or singing (giving voice), is the innate property of children. Although, like language, music carries within it the distinct accent or dialect as well as the period in time from which it was born, it is also a universal language that can be understood by all who have ears to hear.

Music has an infinite capacity to affect brain and body. It can act as a unifying force and a vehicle by which other skills can be developed, enjoyed, and understood. As such, music can be a powerful means of learning.

7. Of Many Minds

'When I was a child, I spoke like a child,
I thought like a child, I reasoned like a child; when I became
an adult,
I put an end to childish ways.'

Corinthians I.14:11

As we have seen, brain development is a continuous process of elaboration, adaptation, organization, and change. Before the development of modern scanning equipment most of our knowledge of brain specialization was largely gleaned from cases of brain injury or progressive disease in which destruction of a particular site in the brain resulted in a set of symptoms that were specific to the affected area of the brain. In other words, our understanding of the healthy brain and nervous system was largely dependent on the investigation of *damaged* tissue – a process of abstraction, which has only revealed a fraction of the story.

In the 1960s Roger Sperry and Ronald Myers carried out a series of experiments on animals in which they severed the fibres of the corpus callosum, the millions of nerve fibres that connect the two cerebral hemispheres. This technique resulted in a split brain, in which the cortical tissue remained intact, but communication between the two sides of the brain was cut off. In this way, it was possible to investigate the functioning of each side of the brain separately. This procedure was later carried out on humans suffering from intractable epilepsy, and provided the foundations for greater understanding of the specialized abilities of the left and right hemispheres, much of which has been confirmed by modern imaging techniques.

In earlier chapters it has been shown that one of the tasks of childhood is to build connections within the brain. It is not only links between higher and lower regions that are important, but also the establishment of connections between the two hemispheres. This is never a simple one-way system, but an interaction of processes whereby rapid development of the cortex (highest centre) facilitates inhibition of lower systems, while practice and *usage* of lower centres builds in connections to the two cerebral hemispheres. This is the period described by the Swiss psychologist Jean Piaget as the sensory-motor period of development. The primitive and postural reflexes act as 'tools of the trade', or mechanisms whereby simple movements start to bring about the long process of integration. It is also during the first three and a half years of life that the cerebellum, a part of the brain involved in the regulation and modulation of controlled movement, undergoes intensive maturation.

The cerebellum acts rather like the fine tuning switch on an old-fashioned radio or television, modulating signals from other centres involved in motor performance to ensure that motor output is precise and well controlled. Strongly influenced by the vestibular system, the cerebellum operates through the postural reflex system for the maintenance of posture and progressive movements such as walking and running at a subconscious or automatic level, but its functions are not confined to motor activity alone. PET scans have shown that higher regions of the cerebellum are involved in many activities related to practice learning: error detection, mental imagery of movements (ideation), judging the time and speed of moving stimuli, rapid shifting of attention between sensory modalities, cognitive operations in three-dimensional space and word association.[38] In other words, the cerebellum is involved in many cognitive operations which have a motor component, particularly those skills that are developed through practice.

Although the cerebellum has no 'cognitive' memory of its own, it is a key player in skills that require muscular memory and practice-related learning, such as playing a musical instrument or learning to touch-type. If you ask a skilled typist to describe where the various characters are on a keyboard, she will often have to use her fingers in order to locate them; this is an example of muscular memory. The cerebellum has also been shown to be involved in sequencing tasks such as learning multiplication tables, days of the weeks, months of the year, and in timing. During the early stages of learning such skills, the cerebellum is shown to be very active, but with practice, the amount of activity decreases.

The cerebellum assists the cortex in laying down and refining the sensory-motor aspects of certain skills so that physical action can become automatic and the cortex is free to concentrate on cognitive and adaptive functions. The foundations for these abilities are laid in the first three and a half years of life at the same time that balance, posture, and basic motor skills are being learned.

What are the Implications of Different Stages of Brain Development for Education?

Although learning can take place at any stage in development, it is more efficient if it coincides with the time of neurological 'readiness'. Just as the developing foetus is most vulnerable at times of rapid development, so learning is enhanced if it coincides with a time of rapid elaboration and change.

The thalidomide tragedy provides an example of how potent any form of intervention can be (good or bad) if it occurs at a period of rapid developmental change. One of the reasons why it took some time before thalidomide was identified as the rogue that lay behind a group of children born with limb deformities was because many mothers took thalidomide in pregnancy and went on to give birth to normal children. It was only in cases where the mother took the drug at the *time* in pregnancy when the limb buds were developing that such devastating results occurred. In other words, it was *when* the drug was used rather than use of the drug *per se* that prevented the limbs from developing.

The 'Tree of Knowledge' Figure 31 provides a model to show when various parts of the brain pass through optimum times of learning readiness.

As discussed in Chapter 6, development of the right hemisphere proceeds slightly ahead of the left hemisphere up to about 7 years of age, with a major period of development taking place between 4 and 7 years. The right hemisphere is generally slightly larger than the left and has more downward connections than the left, linking it to the areas involved in basic functions such as control of movement, sensory processing, emotion, memory, and hormonal regulation (limbic system). In this sense the right brain could be called the 'feeling' side of the brain – the side that is most closely in touch with emotions and survival functions. The right brain 'knows' things, recognizes 'gut feelings', but cannot easily articulate them in verbal language because it is limited in its capacity to describe in words what it feels – superior centres for speech and language being located in the left hemisphere.

Despite its linguistic limitations, the right brain has other specialized abilities. It is primarily visual in the way that it processes information, and it views situations holistically. It is the

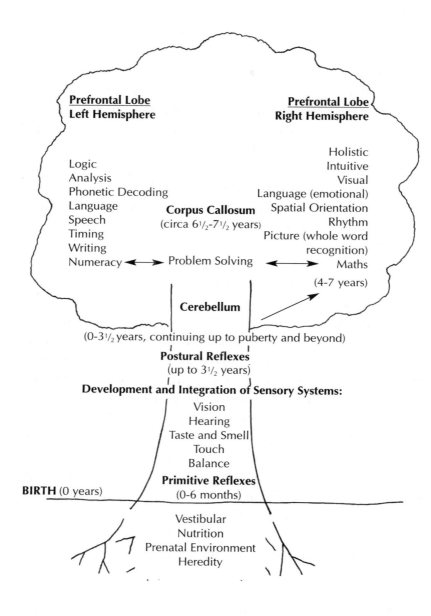

Figure 31. The Tree of Knowledge:
Stages of Maturation in the Central Nervous System (Goddard 2002)

expert in solving visual-spatial problems, jigsaw puzzles, and mazes, and it is good at drawing. In fact, in her book *Drawing on the Right Side of the Brain*, Betty Edwards suggests that if only we could block off interference from the left side, we could all be good artists. The right brain has a natural ability to recognize and copy musical melodies and rhythm; it is intuitive, creative, and in some ways 'child like' in the way that it views the world. Its holistic nature means that it can view situations unfettered by the constraints of time, logic, and realism. In other words, it is the part of the brain that can indulge in fantasy, see beyond what it is, and has a visionary ability all of its own.

The years of optimum right-hemisphere development are years when learning is still strongly linked to sensory-motor activity. Sequences of information like the alphabet or multiplication tables can be memorized easily if they are learned with movement, or put into rhyme, rhythm, or song. The child may not understand the *meaning* of what it has learned, but the information is stored and available when needed at a later date.

This is the time in development when children can see pictures in the clouds. I can still remember myself as a small child sitting on the staircase at home, fascinated by the shapes that were fashioned in chips in the paintwork on the banisters – one formed a wolf's head; another a tree. Astronomers do the same with the stars. In the right brain, even whole words are processed more like pictures than words. The 'look/say' method of teaching a child to read shows the 'word-picture' to the right brain while the left side of the brain registers the sounds. Later on, when phonics are taught, the left brain becomes increasingly active in breaking words down, analysing the sounds, and rebuilding words from individual letters.

This is the time for make-believe, dressing up, creating castles in the air, and searching for fairies at the bottom of the garden. Although belief in the impossible becomes tempered with time, it should never entirely desert us. It is part of the magic of childhood, and underlies some of the greatest works and acts of creativity achieved by humankind.

Ancient cultures frequently place more value on the wisdom of the right side of the brain. Amongst the aborigines of Australia, for example, the concept of 'the Dreaming' was born amongst a migrant people who grafted symbolic meaning on to the landscape that sustained them. Every woman was born with her own unique 'songline'. The songline was a symbol that acted as her talisman for life. The symbol might be a bird or a particular tree whose shape and form she was able to find anywhere in the landscape around her. If she was lost in the bush, she would seek out her symbol, and her songline would lead her in the right direction. It could be seen in the sky, a copse of trees, an animal, or a person's shadow, and it provided continuity and security throughout her life. The Aboriginal 'Dreaming Landscape' is an embodiment of mystical realities not easily explained by language – a faith in visionary intuition which is able to 'make sense' of the world without the need for verbal reasoning.

In a very different culture, one artist of the French Impressionist movement also used a similar concept for a different purpose. 'In everything', said Cézanne, 'there can be found a sphere, a cylinder or a cone.' The ability to find these uniform shapes in all matter helped him to reproduce form in drawing and painting. In other words, it was a way of seeing the world, and of finding continuity in an ever-changing environment. Both the songline of the Aborigine, and the style of an artist or musical composer, carry within them a 'signature'. This signature theme is the composer's unique contribution to the music or painting that he creates – it is like a trademark or patent that he stamps on his composition from which the educated ear or eye can identify the master behind the work.

Whilst there may be various techniques that the artist employs to achieve his goal, the idiom that underlies the whole is more than just the sum of carefully constructed artistic devices; it is the *meaning* that lies within the gestalt.

The right side of the brain is also more prone to fear, sadness, anxiety, and pessimism. If an adult has a stroke on the left side of the brain, leaving the right brain free rein, the patient is often overly aware of the awfulness of what has happened to them, takes a pessimistic view of the future, and is prone to depression. Patients who suffer right-hemisphere damage are the opposite, often blissfully unaware of the impact of their injury or their own shortcomings, and they view the world with an optimism totally unsupported by the facts of life.

The left hemisphere, on the other hand, is logical and analytical. If it is unable to solve a problem immediately, it will attempt to break it down and analyse the pieces until it can make sense of them. Specialist areas for decoding auditory information, speech, and language are located in the left hemisphere, as is the *executive* sense of time, but a sense of time is also linked to efficient vestibular/cerebellar functioning. Once again, lower centres of the brain support the cerebral cortex in its more specialized abilities.

While the right brain is inherently musical, the left hemisphere becomes more involved in processing music as a result of musical training. Indeed, a number of studies have shown a greater degree of symmetry in the brains of professional musicians than non-musicians, indicating increased left-hemisphere involvement in musical performance – the right side providing the natural 'musicality' of the individual, and the left side contributing to the technique and detail of performance. But of course, the story is much more complicated than this. Once again, the cerebellum must be recruited in the automatization of the muscular movements required for performance; the vestibular system contributes to the sense of rhythm, time, and spatial aspects of music, while the left hemisphere is particularly proficient at decoding fast sounds. In other words, the executive functions of the two hemispheres are co-dependent with lower centres, located in Figure 31 as the roots and the trunk of the Tree of Knowledge. These are areas of the brain that are 'primed' through sensory-motor experience.

Most functions require cooperation between the two hemispheres. This is made possible through the corpus callosum, which consists of millions of nerve fibres, which act rather like telephone wires through which information is exchanged back and forth in both directions. Many interchanges can take place within a fraction of a second, allowing the two sides to work together in perfect harmony. The corpus callosum has a dual function: to facilitate communication between the two halves of the brain, but also, at times, to screen one side from the activity of the other. Screening is important to prevent too much 'interference' from one side with the other, so that increased specialization of function can occur. If there is excessive cross-talk between the two sides, it can affect the ability to focus attention (grasshopper brain), and result in 'overflow'. A classic example of overflow can be seen in the old game of trying to pat your head and rub your tummy at the same time. The dominant hemisphere will try to insist that the other side follows its lead. The other side can only perform a separate task if it temporarily disassociates itself from its more dominant partner and is allowed to have a mind of its own.

Some activities actually require the dominant hemisphere to suspend supremacy. When learning to juggle, for example, it is tempting to lead with the dominant hand. In order to be successful, both hands (and both sides of the brain) need to act as equal partners. I only learned to juggle in my forties, when a circus performer forbade me to start with my right hand – only then was I able to develop a fluent rhythm between both sides of the body.

Between 6¹/₂ and 8 years of age a major period of myelination takes place, in which connections between the vestibular system, the cerebellum, and the corpus callosum are strengthened. This is the same time in development when lateral preference should become established. The right-handed child, for example, should naturally use their right eye at far and near distance, right foot for kicking a ball and climbing upstairs (vice versa for the left-handed child), and right ear for processing the sounds of speech. The establishment of a preferred side reflects increased organization and specialization within the higher reaches of the brain.

Many people remain cross-lateral into adult life without ill-effect, but a well lateralized brain is a more organized brain, allowing greater efficiency of processing and performance as circuits become specialized for particular tasks. Before laterality becomes established, *both* sides of the brain are involved in the learning of skills, often vying for supremacy rather like quarrelsome children who risk losing the plot in the argument over who is best. If one side consistently wins the argument, connections to that side become stronger with time, and increased specialization results. However, we should never lose sight of the fact that *both* sides of the brain are involved in the period of *entrainment*, and that the partner that secedes supremacy to the other side continues to provide a supporting, if secondary, role.

In the early years, the development of language is a bilateral process with the right hemisphere playing an important part in the training of non-verbal aspects of language – meaning, gesture, eye contact, body language, visualization, and interpretation of tone: aspects described as 'paralanguage'. The left side is involved in the decoding of sounds, particularly fast sounds and rapid changes of frequency, timing, and sequential organization. The journey toward articulate speech, which eventually culminates in the left hemisphere for the majority of people, begins as a dual brain process. This, in turn, has important implications for the teaching of literacy skills.

By referring back to the 'Tree of Knowledge' (see Figure 31), it can be used as a model, to show stages of readiness for different types of learning. Chronological age is of secondary importance; of primary importance is the *developmental level of the individual child*. If teaching is aimed at the child's developmental level, then effective learning will result.

With this model in mind, what sort of activities can be harnessed to encourage learning at different stages of development?

Development, Learning Readiness, and Play

1. **Training the Primitive Reflexes (0-6 months) and Postural Reflexes (0-3$\frac{1}{2}$ years)** – Training of Postural Control and Sensory Integration through Movement

   Vestibular Stimulation
   Types of movement (passive)
   • Gentle rocking movements provided by a swinging cradle, rocking-chair, mother's movements when feeding.
   • Being pushed in the pram (horizontal), being carried, pushed in a buggy (semi-upright), riding in the car.

   Vestibular-Tactile-Proprioceptive
   • Learning to hold the head up when lying on the tummy and the back
   • Learning to support weight on the forearms as head control develops
   • Kicking movements (help the baby to know its own body length)
   • Reaching movements (hand/eye coordination)

- Feeding movements (developing control of the oral region, facial muscles, swallowing, breathing, and near-point vision)
- Increased postural control results in mastery of the body position in the different planes of gravity – rolling, sitting, crawling, creeping, and standing
- Toward the end of the first year, can put gestures to sounds, e.g. 'bye bye'. Enjoys games such as 'pat-a-cake'

Tactile
Movements involved in:
- Feeding
- Body contact and movement against a supporting surface, weight bearing and shifting of weight from one part of the body to another as muscular strength increases
- Movement of the body – grasping, sucking, learning how to let go of an object, placing objects in the mouth for exploration

Auditory
- Sound of mother's voice
- Sound of own voice – cooing and babbling
- Sounds of the environment
- Tuning in to the sounds of speech
- *Talk* to your child
- Sing, recite nursery rhymes, and *read* to your child. The general sounds will become so familiar that at a later age your child can join in with you.

Visual
Develops in cooperation with vestibular and motor skills:
- Reaching – hand-to-mouth activities, hand to foot
- Bringing objects to the midline

- Passing objects from hand to hand
- Following (tracking) moving objects
- Hand/eye coordination involved in crawling, creeping on hands and knees (helps to develop depth perception and ability to cross the midline with the eyes)

2. **Improving Postural Control** – Helping the cerebellum

1–3 Years – Practice of Postural Control, Balance and Motor Skills
- Push-along toys
- Wants to explore everything in sight!
- Climbing activities
- Rock and ride-along toys, e.g. rocking-horse, train/truck on wheels
- Toys that *move* – ball, car
- Building and shape sorting toys, e.g. blocks
- Walking, running, and rough-and-tumble play

2-4 Years – Increasing use of more complex equipment
- Ride-along toys that can be propelled with feet on the ground or pedals
- Floor play with bricks, boxes, wooden train, dolls, spinning-top
- Simple climbing equipment, slide
- Live music, tapes or CDs of nursery rhymes and songs with actions
- Moulding and modelling activities – plasticine, play dough, sand play, baking with Mum, playing with paint, water play
- Games in the park – roundabouts, swings, slides, see-saws
- Make-believe, dressing up
- *Talk* to your child

- Sing and read to your child; encourage your child to sing with you

3. **Dual Carriageway** – Training both sides of the brain

   4-7 years: Teaching through the Senses – Learning with the Body
   Give a physical activity for each new concept to which your child is introduced:
   - 'Tune in' your child's ears for reading with simple songs (right brain)
   - Encourage your child to 'say aloud' (not read) with you well-known stories as you read them (left brain)
   - Devise movement games, chants, or songs to help memorize sequential information (tables, days of the week, etc.) (right brain)
   - Play physical games to develop spatial awareness – reaching for up, down, touch the toes crossing the midline, free movement in space, rolling down a slope, climbing (both hemispheres)
   - Use of more advanced apparatus – trampoline, bouncy balls, wobble boards, scooter boards, learning to ride a bicycle.

In a personal communication (2003), Professor Lyelle Palmer points out that, in some persons (true 'lefties'), the functions of the two cerebral hemispheres are reversed. When we speak of right- or left-hemisphere skills/abilities we are speaking of left-hemisphere language dominance in 95+ per cent of the population who are usually (but not always) right handed. For 2-3 per cent of the population the right hemisphere is the language hemisphere and the left hemisphere is the tonal hemisphere. Some have said that these persons are the only ones in their right mind. My point is that when we speak of dominance, language hemispheric dominance is the important issue in understanding academic problems. For example, the two visual fields process information in different ways: the right visual field is sensed by the nasal retinal field of the right eye that sends two-thirds of the ocular signal to the left hemisphere. The opposite is true of the left visual field – the right half of the right-eye retina sends one-third of the retinal signal to the right hemisphere. These proportions are reversed in the left eye. Such differences can affect the way that visual symbols are processed linguistically.

8. Feeding, Growth, and the Brain

> 'Let food be your medicine and medicine be your food .'
> Hippocrates

In most creatures, the brain is located near the entrance to the gut, and in some simple life forms the mechanisms for feeding and movement are part of the same system. Echinoderms, for example (a group of sea animals, which include the sand dollar, sea urchin, starfish, and sea lily), are equipped with numerous tiny tube feet, which project from the lower surface of the body, ending with a suction cup. These tube feet are part of a water-vascular system, which is involved in movement, respiration, and food capture.

Sea water enters through an opening on the upper surface of the body and is conducted through a ring canal, which encircles the oesophagus (feeding tube), from where a series of radial canals branch off. The radial canals conduct water down to the tube feet, each of which is controlled by a muscular squeeze bulb. Contraction of the squeeze bulb pushes water into the tube foot, forcing it to extend. This simple nervous system provides a means for propulsion, ingesting and eliminating food as well as gas exchange.

These simple life forms provide an example of how the entrance to the gut or the mouth is the seed kernel from which more complex activities evolve. In Chapter 3 we have seen how activity associated with feeding, such as rooting and sucking, leads into more complex functions. In the human infant, when sucking ceases to be the sole form of nourishment as weaning takes place, the first teeth start to appear. The development and refinement of dentition has been a major feature in the development of mammals, and particularly primates. The development of a combination of canine teeth (for tearing), incisors (for cutting), and molars (for grinding) has allowed humankind in particular to extend the scope and variety of foods that it can digest. Animals with large brains require an enormous amount of nourishment to sustain brain growth and function. In ancient man, three factors combined to make this possible.

1. Change in diet, which included increased consumption of animal products in addition to available plant resources, provided high quality proteins containing all the essential amino acids in the right percentages. Amino acids are the sub-units from which proteins are made. The introduction of meat and other animal products into the diet provided a secure source of high quality protein, of which a by-product was the development of larger brains. Increased protein intake coincided with the period of most prodigious brain development, particularly development of the cortex.

2. Early man obtained much of his meat, not by killing live animals but by scavenging from the pickings of other predators. What was really needed for efficient utilization of meat was sharp tools for butchering. Tool-making also played a role in the evolution of the human brain; refinement of hand skills contributed to organization within the nervous

system and specialization within the brain itself. The making and utilization of tools is associated with forward planning and independent use of the two sides of the body.

3. Alteration in diet resulted in the development of larger brains and smaller teeth, an adaptation that required a gradual change of upper and lower jaw positions. The position of the jaw and the 'bite' has a major influence on speech production. The early feeding experiences of the human infant – sucking, pushing with the tongue, chewing, grinding, and swallowing – are important not only for developing the mechanical aspects of later speech but also in stimulating enzymes for the breakdown of food in the stomach and movement of the peristaltic gut.

Before the dawn of fast food it used to be said that each mouthful should be chewed at least 40 times before swallowing. Today, this is cynically regarded as old-fashioned poppycock, but like many old wives' tales it had a sound basis in observation and experience. The action of chewing stimulates movement in the small intestine, where absorption takes place. Digestion, like sensory awareness, begins with the mouth.

In addition to protein and amino acids, which play a vital role in expression of the genes, fats provide another major constituent of nervous system tissue. An alternative hypothesis to the long-held theory that the major distinctions between Ape and Man took place when the apes were forced to leave the forest for the savannah is that humans, once upon a time, were swimming apes who adapted to live both in water and on land. This theory, described by Elaine Morgan in *The Aquatic Ape* and *The Scars of Evolution*, develops Alister Hardy's hypothesis that bipedalism (standing on two feet rather than four) occurred as a progression from walking on the hind legs, which evolved as a means of keeping the head above water. In other words, humans began as wading animals. The 'aquatic origins' hypothesis is still disputed by anthropologists, but it does gather strength when we look at some of the features that distinguish Man from Ape, such as loss of body hair, volitional breathing, shedding of tears, manual dexterity, migration of the vagina to a sheltered site within the body, a descended larynx, the acquisition of speech, and being born with a hefty deposit of subcutaneous fat – all features shared by marine mammals. *Why* is the human infant born with so much fat?

Good Fats and Bad Fats

No other primate is born with such a ratio of body fat combined with feeble muscle tone. On the other hand, high deposits of fat are an advantage to aquatic animals in maintaining warmth and buoyancy and streamlined movement through the water. Build-up of fat seems to be a last-minute occurrence, which occurs in the final weeks of pregnancy. Michael Crawford (cited in Morgan, 1994) suggested that 'the building of brain tissue demands a one-to-one balance between Omega 3 and Omega 6 fatty acids. Omega-3 fatty acids are relatively scarce in the land food chain, but predominate in the marine food chain.' It is possible that at one time in our ancestral history, seafood formed a much larger proportion of the diet than in modern times.

Essential fatty acids are necessary in helping to form the membrane barrier that surrounds the cells and in formation of the myelin sheath – the fatty coating that surrounds certain nerve pathways facilitating faster transmission of information along the nerve fibre – and rapidly growing human brains are voracious in their need for specific fats. The store of fat that is laid down before birth may well be providing a storehouse for the first years of life, when brain growth, myelination, and elaboration occur at an explosive rate.

Low-birth-weight babies have a higher incidence of infant mortality and are more prone to neurological impairment. They are also at higher risk of diseases such as heart disease, diabetes, and renal failure in later life. Maternal under-nourishment or placental insufficiency stunts growth before birth, affecting the laying down of deposits of subcutaneous fat in the final weeks of pregnancy. It may also affect the 'programming' of the child's metabolism in later life. Insulin-producing cells in the pancreas, for example, are over-worked in low-birth-weight babies, making them more susceptible to diabetes in later life and prone to obesity in adulthood.[39]

The importance of specific fats for brain development seems at first glance to be contradicted by the fact that human breast milk is relatively low in fat content compared to cow's milk. Breast milk is, however, high in essential fatty acids (EFAs), which are not as plentiful in formula milk. The modern Western diet contains a surfeit of animal fats but is often low in the essential fatty acids that are found in high concentrations in fish oils and certain unprocessed vegetable oils.

Essential fatty acids play a role in many aspects of growth, development, and behaviour, helping to:[40]

- Form the membrane barrier that surrounds the cells;
- Determining fluidity and chemical reactivity of membranes;
- Increasing oxidation rate, metabolic rate, and energy levels;
- Serving as starting material for hormone-like substances – prostaglandins that are involved in the regulation of blood pressure, platelet stickiness, and kidney function;
- Are precursors to derivatives like DHA, which are needed by the most active tissues – brain, retina, adrenal glands, and testes;
- Help the immune system to fight infections and help to prevent the development of allergies.

Essential fatty acids are difficult for the body to store and are easily destroyed by light, air, and heat – frying and deep-frying are particularly destructive. 'To unfold their benefits, EFAs must be fresh, protected from destruction by light, oxygen and heat *and accompanied by the minerals and vitamins required for their metabolism in the body.* An adequate supply of healing fats is more important to health than the avoidance of killer fats.'[41]

Fads and fashions often turn a complete circle with the passage of time. At the beginning of the twenty-first century, we are just emerging from a period of being told that a low fat diet is good for the heart, but new findings are beginning to contradict this rather simplistic view. It is now being discovered that certain individuals who eat a diet with a relatively high fat content actually have lower cholesterol levels. The general consensus at the time of writing is that a healthy diet is not composed of 'good' and 'bad' foods, but rather depends on a *balance* between different food groups, different types of fat, climate, and life-style. In 1898, Halleck observed that, 'if all we drank was skimmed milk, then we would have skimmed milk thoughts'! Certain fats are, after all, important for the development of brain and body tissue.

Lack of vitamin and mineral co-factors, particularly zinc, magnesium, and vitamins B3, B6, and C, prevents synthesis of fatty acids, all of which points to the importance of a varied and healthy diet at all times of life, but particularly *prior* to and during pregnancy and breast-feeding – times when modern women are sometimes tempted to restrict their diet for fear of excessive weight gain. It also reminds us of the old motto that, when possible, 'Breast is best'. Nature has poured into breast milk just the right blend and balance of nutrients to provide for the growth not only of a healthy body, but also a healthy brain. Breast milk contains the ideal ratio of 'healthy' bacteria and flora, which help to prime the immune system and the gut for the efficient absorption of essential nutrients. Factors contained within breast milk also help to provide defence against infection in the first months of life, and protection against the development of allergies in later life. Breast-feeding also stimulates increase in maternal levels of the hormone oxytocin, which is thought to play a chemical role in the bonding process. More about oxytocin a little later.

A brief journey through some of the vitamins, minerals, and trace elements that combine to act as precursors for the synthesis of hormones and biochemical functioning might be helpful in understanding why a *varied* diet is so important for optimum health. The nervous system depends upon biochemical factors for efficient functioning.

Zinc

The amount of zinc needed by the body is actually very small, but as with all micro-nutrients, deficiency of even these small amounts can have a profound effect on the functioning of the system as a whole.

Zinc is involved in many metabolic processes in plants and animals. It acts as a catalyst in electron transfer from one molecule to another, and it is essential for all protein synthesis and the way in which the body handles carbohydrates and fats. It is necessary for the utilization of some vitamins and for the formation of blood, enzymes, and hormones. It has long been known to promote wound healing – hence the high zinc content of various skin lotions such as zinc and castor oil cream used for the prevention and treatment of nappy rash, calamine lotion, and Fuller's Earth Cream. Zinc-infused bandages are also used for the treatment of severe eczema. It is involved in the functioning of the immune system (zinc is often an ingredient of remedies for colds and sore throats such as zinc and vitamin C lozenges), and is involved in reproductive processes in both sexes.

Males need up to five times as much zinc as females *in utero* for the formation of the testes.[42] Females need increased zinc resources once the ovaries start to function at about 9 years of age when zinc is required with other co-factors for the synthesis of various hormones. Because of the different developmental stages at which zinc is required between the sexes, *symptoms* of zinc deficiency may show up in a different form according to the age and sex of the child.

Zinc is also necessary for the formation of DNA and RNA – the genetic molecules of life. It is therefore a factor in the expression of genetic potential, and deficiency can be passed on from one generation to the next. In her book *Sexual Chemistry*, Ellen Grant suggests that a number of diseases hitherto considered to be genetic in origin may be related to familial zinc deficiency, which then affects the expression of genetic potential within members of the same family.

Zinc is an essential component of all aspects of development. It is necessary for sperm production, fertility, successful outcome of pregnancy, and maternal behaviour. A number of studies carried out on rats have shown that rats fed zinc-deficient diets during pregnancy failed to 'mother' their offspring: they ignored or rejected their young, and failed either to groom or to feed their babies normally. Rat pups reared on a diet with an inadequate supply of zinc showed signs of lethargy, reduced weight gain, inferior performance on two measures of learning ability, and increase in emotionality when compared to rat pups who had been reared on a zinc-enriched diet.[43]

Growth, sexual maturity, learning ability, stress resistance, and behavioural control have all been linked to zinc status in the body.[44] Amongst some of the behavioural changes noted in medical literature are depression, sensitivity to light, impaired sense of taste and smell, anorexia and bulimia nervosa, and impaired concentration. Low zinc levels have also been noted amongst children seen at the Institute for Neuro-Physiological Psychology in Chester who were suffering from post-viral malaise.

The Foresight organization, which was set up to promote pre-conceptual care, has spent over 20 years researching into the effects of vitamin, mineral, and trace element deficiencies on fertility, pregnancy outcome, and children who manifest learning difficulties and hyperactivity. Foresight has observed that zinc deficiency seems to be associated with,

> 'poor growth and general development both before and after birth, colic and diarrhoea, poor sucking, late teething and other milestones and generally retarded development both physically and mentally. Hyperactivity, dyslexia and behaviour problems mar the school career and general growth, and puberty may be delayed and/or incomplete.'

They go on to note that,

> 'if zinc deficiency is present at birth the labour may be difficult and delayed, breast feeding may be difficult to establish, bonding may not take place and post-partum depression may set in. Post-partum depression and lactation failure have been found empirically to respond well to zinc and vitamin B supplementation.'[45]

Zinc deficiency seems to be a growing problem in the world for a number of reasons. Modern intensive farming methods add a number of fertilizers to the soil, all of which help to produce abundant and apparently flourishing crops. Zinc, however, is not one of the substances regularly put back *in* to the soil. In the days of crop rotation, or when a field lay fallow, the soil had time to regenerate zinc supply for the production of the next crop. In this way, every yield contained an adequate supply of zinc. Many of the plants that we now eat, and the animal products that have fed from them, come from soil where the zinc content was low. However 'healthy' the diet, it is apparently getting more difficult to ensure an adequate intake of zinc. The modern need to obtain a faster and bigger profit threatens the age-old concept of husbandry, which originally had a triple meaning, 'to dwell, to farm and to care for'.

Zinc, lead, and cadmium act as antagonists. If lead or cadmium is present in high concentrations (lead may be present in the water pipes of old buildings, or in areas where there is heavy traffic pollution; cadmium is present in cigarettes), zinc absorption is compromised – toxic levels of lead and cadmium rise while zinc falls. Equally, zinc deficiency can allow levels of other less desirable trace elements to rise in the body. In the days when water was carried in zinc buckets, the balance was naturally maintained. Although plastic pipes may be more hygienic, they do not replenish zinc in the water![46]

Highly processed foods such as white bread and sugar lose much of their zinc concentration during processing, while at the other end of the spectrum, excessive consumption of bran and fibre can inhibit the absorption of zinc. Excessive alcohol consumption, smoking, stress, and the contraceptive pill can all interfere with zinc metabolism. Zinc, together with chromium, helps to regulate blood glucose levels. Stable blood sugar levels are necessary for the maintenance of concentration, rational thinking, and impulse control.

It would be wrong to see zinc as the answer to all ills. It does, however, provide an *example* of how important it is to maintain a wide range of individual elements in feeding habits. Shortage of one element can affect the way the body utilizes many others.

Some sources of zinc

Lean meat, oysters, ginger root, oats, egg yolk, whole wheat and rye, haddock, shrimps and tuna, split peas, chicken, lentils, cauliflower, spinach, and cabbage. Spices such as black pepper, paprika, chilli powder, and cinnamon are also good sources of zinc.

Magnesium

Magnesium is used by the body for many purposes, often working in conjunction with calcium and phosphorus. Some 70 per cent of the body's supply of magnesium is contained within the teeth and the bones, but it is also an important constituent of the cells, soft tissues, and fluid surrounding the cells. Its main function is to activate certain enzymes, especially those enzymes involved in carbohydrate metabolism, and also to maintain the electrical potential across nerve and cell membranes and to assist in protein formation and storage and release of energy.

Magnesium and calcium act as antagonists, operating together to create a perfect balance. In nerve cells, for example, calcium acts as the stimulator while magnesium is a relaxant. The same is true for the functioning of the heart. Calcium is responsible for heart contraction, while magnesium is responsible for relaxation, which leads into the next pumping action or contraction. Hence, certain medications for heart disease operate by inhibiting the action of calcium and reducing arterial spasm. Other functions of magnesium include lowering of cholesterol levels in the blood, acting as an anti-thrombotic agent, helping to protect nerve and muscle functions against cramp, and ridding the body of excess sodium (salt). Psychologically it has a calming effect and helps to protect against over-reaction to stimuli.

Magnesium deficiency can result in a variety of symptoms, which include: over-anxiety, irritability, labile emotions, craving for sweets and alcohol, and stiffness of fine muscle movements.

Some sources of magnesium

Kelp, fresh green peas, whole grains, nuts, and seeds.

Calcium

Calcium is the most abundant mineral in the body. Most people are aware that calcium is important for healthy bones and teeth, but calcium is necessary for much more besides. It is needed for transmission of nerve impulses, blood clotting, heart function, acid-alkaline balance in the blood, muscle growth, and the activation of enzymes that transport nutrients through cell membranes. If calcium levels in the blood start to fall, parathyroid hormone is secreted by the thyroid gland to release calcium from the bone in order maintain blood calcium levels. Calcium levels in the bones and teeth are not permanent but are continuously deposited and removed according to the needs of the body. Calcium deficiency can therefore extract calcium from bones and teeth, a process known as demineralization, which in the long term can lead to osteoporosis and permanent tooth decay.

Calcium deficiency can also affect the functioning of the muscles, nerves, and general growth. Muscle cramps that occur when at rest can be one sign of a low calcium level, as can general nervousness and irritability, because calcium, in its role as a regulator of sodium-potassium levels, has a calming effect on the nerves. (There are of course many other reasons for nervousness and irritability that are *not* connected to low calcium.) Various hormones, particularly oestrogen, help to maintain calcium levels in the body, hence the increased susceptibility to demineralization that can occur in women following the menopause.

If calcium levels are low in childhood, growth may be stunted, and in extreme cases rickets can develop. Vitamin D is required for calcium to be absorbed and utilized by the body. Vitamin D is found in cod liver oil, dairy products, and *sunlight*.

Keith Eaton,[47] a medical consultant who specializes in nutrition, told a story about two groups of families who came to live in the UK from Asia. One family went to live in London, the other in the north of England. When some of the children living in the north started to show signs of rickets, doctors started to investigate whether both groups had changed their diet when they came to the United Kingdom, or whether they had brought their indigenous diet with them. When they found that both groups followed much the same diet, they were somewhat flummoxed as to the cause of illness in only one of the groups. It took some time before they realized that the family in the south received about 15-20 minutes of extra sunlight a day, and this additional sunlight was just sufficient to maintain their vitamin D levels so that calcium balance could be maintained.

Research in the 1990s[48] sought to measure zones on the earth's surface where sunlight provides sufficient vitamin D to maintain human health. The researchers found that the earth's surface could be divided into three areas: (1) the tropics, (2) the sub-tropics and temperate zones, and (3) the circumpolar regions north and south of 45 degrees latitude. They found that in zone 2 there was at least one month of the year when the climate did not provide enough sunlight to sustain vitamin D and dependent calcium levels unless other sources were provided through the diet. In zone 3, supplies are insufficient throughout the year, but potential deficiency is usually compensated for by a diet high in fish.

Furthermore, the required ratio of vitamin D and folate (one of the vitamin B group known to be important for the prevention of neural tube defects such as Spina Bifida in the developing foetus) will depend on skin colour. 'Throughout the world, human skin colour has evolved to be dark enough to prevent sunlight from destroying the nutrient folate, but light enough to foster the production of vitamin D.'[49] Migration from one zone to another without adequate dietary adjustment could, in theory, produce just the type of problem found in the two groups of Asian immigrants to the United Kingdom.

Some sources of calcium

Kelp, Swiss and Cheddar cheese, milk and milk products, leafy green vegetables, citrus fruits, and legumes.

In our modern Western world where it is so easy to transport fresh produce from one part of the world to another, it is possible to eat fresh foods all through the year. Children growing up in an urban environment today have often never known the excitement of the first fresh peas of the summer when they were put on the table; the season for strawberries and cream; and as the strawberry season slowly passed, raspberries ripened to fill the gap. Summer was a feast of fresh berries and vegetables, rich in vitamin C, which would help to build up a store in the body to protect from infection through the winter months. The old traditions of bottling and preserving ensured that these fruits were still available through the winter, and also contained high levels of sugar and fats to help keep the body warm. In the days of cold winters and before the advent of central heating, it was necessary to eat for warmth. Many of the root vegetables that grow in the winter, such as carrots, parsnips, and turnips, contain high levels of carbohydrate, which is important for instant energy and warmth. Thus, there was wisdom in the ecology and traditions of the past – wisdom that is often lost when change takes place at a rapid rate.

One of the joys of going on holiday abroad is the opportunity to sample the local food: imported food never tastes quite the same. I have never forgotten the taste of fresh oranges in North Africa, peaches in Italy, beans in France, or fresh yoghurt and local honey in Greece. These foods that have come straight from the farm have a flavour that cannot be replicated after freezing, travelling, and storage. They come fresh with the taste of the soil from which they grew; and just as with good wine, each area produces a different crop and a different flavour. Whilst the benefits of all-year fresh food have been enormous, eating according to the season or the area in which we dwell is now sadly considered by many to be a somewhat quaint eccentricity.

Manganese

Manganese is only required in small amounts by the body, but it is worthy of mention here because it is one of the trace elements that has been linked to the functioning of the balance mechanism.

Manganese is required for the functioning of several enzymes, energy production, bone and cartilage formation, and protein metabolism. Manganese deficiency has been implicated in birth defects, growth retardation, poor glucose tolerance, inner-ear problems, seizure, irregular heartbeat, weight loss, and behavioural disorders including schizophrenia.

Inadequate maternal or foetal manganese is thought to contribute to behavioural disorders, alteration in formation of the teeth leading to overcrowding, and abnormalities in formation of part of the balance mechanism with effect upon motor control. Rats born of manganese-deficient mothers are ataxic at birth.[50] 'Congenital ataxia* results from an otolith** defect due to manganese deficiency which produced seizures.' Riopelle and Hubbard (note 50) also found that gestation was longer in rhesus monkeys born to mothers who had been fed a manganese-

---

* Ataxia is the loss of coordination resulting in fragmentation of movement or inability to start and stop movement at a set point.
** Otoliths are minute crystalline particles formed from calcite and protein, which are suspended in a gelatinous mass, which forms the membrane into which the cilia of hair cells of the utricle and sacculus project. The particles are under the influence of gravity, and exert traction on the cilia of the hair cells during movements of the head and the body, influencing reflexes. The otoliths are sometimes also referred to as statoconia ('conia' meaning dust or small stones, 'oto' referring to the ear).

deficient diet prior to pregnancy, and despite the increased period of gestation, the infants were defective in response to gravity, clasping, and righting.

Manganese deficiency also lowers the threshold at which seizures may start to occur. Low levels of manganese have an effect upon levels of dopamine. (Dopamine is a neurotransmitter, or chemical substance, which transmits the action of a nerve to a cell, enabling the nerve to carry out its action.) Dopamine has an inhibitory influence on specific motor tracts. When dopamine levels are *reduced*, as in Parkinson's disease, inappropriate motor movements fail to be inhibited, resulting in uncontrollable tremor when at rest. Abnormally *high* levels of dopamine have been found to be present in people suffering from schizophrenia. If certain drugs used to treat schizophrenia such as Reserpine, which operates by reducing the amount of dopamine available in the brain, are used in excess, they start to produce Parkinsonian-like symptoms. Conversely, the drug Ritalin (Methylphenidate), used to treat Attention Deficit Hyperactivity Disorder (ADHD), works by increasing dopamine availability, thereby boosting inhibition and having a regulatory effect on impulsive behaviour. If the dose of Ritalin is too high, schizophrenic-type symptoms can develop.

Manganese deficiency has been implicated in both seizure disorders and schizophrenia, suggesting that it may be an important precursor to dopamine regulation. In theory, manganese deficiency could play a part in a range of disorders such as epilepsy, Attention Deficit Hyperactivity Disorder, and schizophrenia.

In combination with zinc and chromium, manganese helps to maintain stable blood-glucose levels. If manganese levels drop, it affects the functioning of cells in the pancreas where insulin is manufactured. One theory is that manganese deficiency might contribute to the development of diabetes.

Some sources of manganese

Lentils, beans, pecan, almond and brazil nuts, barley, rye, whole wheat, rice, red cabbage, aubergine, dark chocolate, tea, cloves, ginger, thyme, and bay leaves.

Social Context and Eating Patterns

Hardly a day goes by without a newspaper carrying a report on the latest diet and fitness regime for adults, whilst diet and exercise for children take a back-seat despite the fact that the eating patterns that are established in childhood are the ones that usually set a trend for life.

We are hearing growing concerns about a rising tide of obesity in the Western world. It is now suggested that one in four children and one in five adults are obese, and in 2001, following the publication of some of these studies, there was a call by health experts for a nation-wide programme to stop today's children growing into a generation of obese adults. Such findings raise important questions beyond those of simple calorie intake.

Fat is often regarded as a problem of over-nutrition, but it is possible to be overweight and undernourished. As we have seen from the description of some of the micro-nutrients above, each one has a crucial part to play, and deficiency in one area can result in a surfeit elsewhere. Calcium for example, helps to keep lead levels in the body low; zinc helps to protect against raised levels of aluminium and is involved in maintaining the correct ratio of zinc to copper in the blood. Low zinc levels can affect not only appetite, as in anorexia, but also taste, resulting in a child who will only eat a narrow range of bland foods, and who refuses to try the very food groups that would help overcome the underlying deficiency.

Eating habits are not simply about food. Many other factors

are involved, including genetic determination of metabolic rate, early feeding patterns, diet selection, and, in some cases, emotional problems which influence eating habits. However, food is also strongly linked to *social context*, and this is one area over which parents and teachers can exert an influence throughout the learning years. Mealtimes matter.

Biological Factors

It takes up to 20 minutes for the hypothalamus (a specific area of the brain involved in the perception of hunger and satiety, sexual behaviour, and temperature control) to register that enough food has been eaten, and for a child to become conscious of a sense of satiety (fullness). The body's normal response to food is for blood sugar (glucose) and insulin levels to rise. Glucose enters the cells, any excess is stored as fat, and appetite decreases.

Fast foods are exactly what they say they are: foods which are instantly available, eaten quickly, often 'on the hoof', and which generally have a high fat/sugar and refined carbohydrate content. Eaten at speed, the satiety centres do not have enough time to register that the body has had enough, and to respond by switching off the hunger signals before intake exceeds the body's requirements.

High sugar/fat/carbohydrate content foods cause an immediate and rapid rise in blood glucose and insulin levels. If too much insulin is produced, the blood glucose falls too low, which results in a craving for more sugar. It is at this stage that a child will demand a 'quick fix' snack such as a fizzy drink, packet of crisps, or candy bar (one fizzy drink contains the equivalent of seven teaspoons of sugar). This will temporarily solve the sugar crisis, but a similar pattern will recur within 2-3 hours. Sugar craving cycles increase the likelihood of obesity.

Evidence supports the idea that obese individuals secrete

more insulin in response to food and food-related cues than non-obese individuals, and are therefore more sensitive to sensations of hunger. Rapidly changing blood sugar levels can also deplete the body's ability to produce insulin in the long term, which may be one reason why children of 10 and 12 years of age are now developing the type of diabetes which used to be found only in middle-aged adults.

Society has changed in the last generation, not only in the type of food children eat but also the manner in which meals are taken.

Sitting down to a formal meal involves taking time over the meal; formal meals tend to last longer than 20 minutes, giving time for the satiety centres in the brain and the body to recognize that the child has had enough. There were certain advantages to the days when children sat down to formal school meals with a set menu and an adult at the end of each table. Children learned by example the value of regularly spaced balanced meals; they experienced a variety of food types; and they learned basic table manners. Customs such as not speaking with your mouth full were not only for the benefit of other people at the table who do not particularly want to see food revolving around the mouth like the contents of a washing machine! They also encouraged children to spend time chewing their food, helping digestion and slowing down the speed at which food is eaten. It also teaches, by daily example, conversational give-and-take, the taking of turns, and appropriate social behaviour.

Michel Odent points out that during social occasions such as the sharing of meals, or the playing of games together, the production of oxytocin is increased. Oxytocin is the hormone involved in the onset of labour and lactation, and it is increased at times of social interaction and sexual intercourse. In his book *The Scientification of Love*, Odent suggests that oxytocin is a powerful force in the formation and sustaining of social and loving relationships. In a society in which relationship bonds are fragile, it is possible that something as simple as sharing a meal together on a daily basis may help physiologically as well as socially to strengthen the ties that hold us together.

Today, many schools have turned to a cafeteria system. Cafeteria-style feeding places the onus of choice upon the child. Children will tend to select items, which either they know or which taste good to them – too often, these are foods with a refined carbohydrate and high fat content. Canteen feeding also requires that the child select the entire meal in advance, as opposed to deciding after the first course whether the second course is necessary.

Although many families do sit down to formal meals as a matter of routine, there are also an increasing number of children who do not. Many children start the school day without breakfast, which means that they have an over-night fasting level of blood glucose. The body's natural reaction to low blood sugar is to compensate by increasing adrenaline output. Such a biochemical combination can affect attention, concentration, and impulse control. In the long term, a pendulum pattern of high/low blood sugar levels increases irritability, fatigue, and bouts of hyperactivity, reduces energy, and impairs concentration.

A study by a former Chief Superintendent of Police,[51] carried out a number of years ago amongst a prison population, found that a high percentage of the inmates suffered from unstable blood sugar levels. When mealtimes were altered and smaller meals containing slow glucose-releasing foods were given at more frequent intervals, there was a significant reduction in the incidence of aggression and violent outbursts amongst inmates.

The relationship between fluctuating blood sugar levels and aggression is illustrated by the story of a mother who went to see a psychotherapist with her teenage son. She was at her wit's end and had been hospitalized for several months for severe depression. Her depression was the result of months of stress, which had begun when her growing son had started to attack her physically. Neither he nor she understood why the attacks occurred. Social workers were brought in, and the mother was made to feel that the aggression took place because she was a weak parent who had failed to provide consistent discipline for her son. As the attacks grew more frequent and aggressive, she found that she could no longer cope.

The psychotherapist asked her if there was a precipitating event leading up to the attacks. She could think of none, other than that they always took place when he returned home from school. Further questioning revealed that they rarely happened in the holidays. When she was asked to describe the sequence of events in term-time, the mother described how her son came into the house and said that he wanted something to eat. She would always say, 'No'! Your father will be home in an hour and then we will all eat together', whereupon her son would attack her. The therapist suggested that she should try giving him something to eat as soon as he came home and delay the family meal until a little later in the evening. Within just two days the attacks had stopped.

The son was going through a rapid spurt of growth. This growth spurt, combined with the mental energy required in school each day, meant that by the time he was ready to leave school, his blood sugar was at an all-time low. Anyone who has ever seen a diabetic going into a hypoglycaemic state will recognize the symptoms that are a by-product of low blood sugar levels: heightened reactivity, irritability, loss of concentration and impulse control, and in diabetes, eventually sweating, dizziness, and coma. The greatest tragedy was the months of suffering the family had endured when the problem was treated as a purely psychological problem.

Schools can help in a number of ways:

- Ensuring that lunch *and* break times allow sufficient time for every child to sit down to eat;
- Not allowing more than 2-3 hours to elapse between lunch and break times (particularly with younger children);
- Placing emphasis on the importance of breakfast, and the fact that small, regularly spaced meals do not cause excessive weight gain (particularly amongst teenage girls);
- Encouraging discussion sessions about the type of foods which help maintain well-being and helping children to understand how body chemistry can affect the functioning of the mind as well as the body;
- Encouraging children to see mealtimes as social events;
- Helping children to experiment with 'new' tastes and types of food by guiding selection;
- One way to help alleviate the symptoms of reactive blood sugar levels is to eat slow glucose-releasing food at regular intervals. In this way, energy is utilized rather than being stored as fat. Examples of slower-releasing foods are: unrefined carbohydrates such as wholemeal bread and whole-grain cereals, protein, fruit, vegetables, and unsweetened fruit juices.
- Allow sufficient time within the school day for daily physical exercise.

Exercise is also important for the efficient utilization of nutrition because nerve cells are nourished through circulation. In addition to tissue repair, growth, and energy, memory is dependent upon nutrition. Individuals with cold hands and feet (a sign of poor circulation to the extremities) often also complain about poor memory. The process through which nutrition is transported efficiently into the cells is through exercise, hence the expression of 'pumping iron'.

Food is fuel for the brain as well as the body. Today's increase in obesity amongst the young is a social problem as well as a personal problem and potential health risk. Expectant mothers are encouraged to eat well for their unborn child. Children also need continued guidance in selecting, regulating, and developing healthy eating patterns for life. This is also a part of education.

9. Turning Children Around

> 'A well-trained nervous system is the greatest friend a mind can have.'
>
> Halleck, 1898

The main focus of this book so far has been to look at factors in development that can influence the progress of a child during the early years, and to give parents and teachers ideas they can use to give a child the best possible environment in which to grow. In the majority of cases, children develop despite their parents, but sometimes something goes awry early on, and the child exhibits difficulties in academic learning or behaviour at a later age.

We have seen that movement is an essential ingredient for a child's development and capacity to learn, but children of today have less movement opportunities in their daily lives than any previous generation. A number of projects are now pointing the way to relatively simple and inexpensive changes that can help to mould our children's future in a more positive direction.

Two pilot studies carried out in inner-city schools in Leicester and Birmingham, UK[52] have shown significant changes in the reading, writing, and drawing skills of children who have participated in a 10-minute daily regime of physical exercises at school. The exercises are based on movements that children normally make in the first year of life just at the time when important

130

connections are being formed between the developing brain and the body. These same connections are necessary for the control of balance, coordination, and eye movements needed to read and write.

In addition to measuring changes in educational achievement, the studies also asked the class teacher and parents to complete a questionnaire at the beginning and end of the project. The questionnaire covered various aspects of each child's behaviour such as the ability to sit still, pay attention, self-confidence, and so on. The children who had taken part in the project all showed significant gains in these areas.

A different approach was implemented in London in 2002, when the facilities of one of the leading public schools, St Paul's, were made available to young offenders through the summer. Police in Barnes, West London, said that criminal activity declined by more than a third since children from the neighbouring estates joined the sports camp.

Whilst it is tempting to dismiss these changes as simply directed use of free time, and petty crime and vandalism as an outlet for boredom and frustration, different projects involving physical exercise all point to similar conclusions. In North Wales, for example, the Clock Tower Centre runs a scheme in which unemployed youths and young offenders are taught circus skills. David Alexander, one of the directors of the centre, has noticed remarkable changes, not only in balance and coordination, but also in self-esteem, attitude, social integration, and motivation. Circus skills require superb mastery of balance, timing, coordination, and discipline – skills which, at the outset, many of the youngsters did not believe they could acquire. They learned to ride a unicycle (control of balance and bilateral integration), to juggle (left-right integration and cerebellar learning), to tumble, and to clown.

Jonny Kiphard, known to some as the 'Father' of Motology in Germany, started his career in movement as a circus clown. When he was Professor at the Department of Prevention and

Rehabilitation through Sport, University of Frankfurt, his hobbies were listed as: yoga, acrobatics, tumbling, circus clowning, miming, juggling, conjuring (magic), music, playing, and enjoying life. Despite being a widely respected academic and innovator in the field of movement education, when he worked with children, he still dressed up as a clown. He found that children could relate to and empathize with a clown who shared all their problems with balance, bewilderment in an adult world, and a desire to impress, whereas a doctor made them feel shy and inhibited. The paradox is that clowns usually have superb control of balance (falling over is the first lesson in standing up), together with remarkable observation of the quirks and body language of the people around them. How else could they mimic and mime human emotions with such eloquence, pathos, and good humour?

It is well recognized that physical play is a necessary part of development in all healthy mammals, and that rough-and-tumble activity seems to be a spontaneous urge stimulated from within the nervous system itself. Panksepp[53] suggests that

> 'play probably has many beneficial effects for both the brain and the body, including the facilitation of certain kinds of learning and various physical skills. At the other extreme, deprivation of sensory experience results in disintegration and abnormal behaviours. Play may allow young animals to be effectively assimilated into the structures of society through various mechanisms from learning who can bully whom, developing cooperative relationships, courting, and parenting skills, as well as the recruitment of various types of emotion. Play networks may help stitch individuals into the social fabric that is the staging ground for their lives.'

Under conditions of social isolation, separation, hunger, fear, anger, or anxiety, play activity is markedly reduced or absent.

Organizers and leaders of outdoor adventure centres also recognize that, given physical responsibility for self or others, such as sailing, abseiling, or climbing a rock face, self-confidence and social responsibility rapidly develop, even in youngsters who had neither belief in their own ability, nor desire to participate, at the outset of the activity. Something happens to attention, behaviour, and motivation when children and young people become *active*. All of which raises a question, 'Where do children of today have space to play?'. Outside of the leafy suburbs, this is a very real and growing problem. Walk through many of our major towns and cities and count just how many green areas you can find within walking distance of family housing where children can engage in *free* physical play.

In many European countries the situation is different. In the evenings, the town square is closed to traffic; families can eat out and 'promenade' in relative safety, and families are welcomed in the smartest restaurants. When I was on holiday once, a local taxi driver in Palma de Majorca pointed out one of the main parks, stressing that it is always patrolled by security guards during opening hours for the protection of both the park and the public. In the United Kingdom, we think nothing of employing security guards for the protection of property – how much more valuable are our children? Recent studies have shown that in the fight against street crime, street *lighting* is more effective than the installation of close-circuit TV, and in countries where there is a police presence on the street, city crime is reduced. In other words, *physical presence* is the most effective security device of all.

Space to Play

A number of years ago one of the founders of 'Toddler Kindy Gymberoo' in Australia was visiting the United Kingdom. Toddler Kindy Gymberoo was set up to encourage parents to provide appropriate exercise and movement opportunities for their children in the first years of life – a sort of super Tumble Tots. Sitting over dinner one evening, she remarked, 'I don't know how any of your children grow up normal in the UK – in the cities your houses are tiny, your gardens are small, and there is hardly any municipal space where children can play.'

This was certainly a problem when my children were growing up living in the centre of a small city in the North West of England. My three children were born within the space of four years, so wherever one went, we all went. When the youngest was three, we moved from the country where we had an endless choice of quiet country lanes to saunter along, riding on toys or pulling them along behind us, to live in a city with a very small garden where the nearest playground was one mile away. The idea of walking these three pairs of very short legs and equally independent minds along a busy street for one mile before play, and back again afterwards, was never very appealing. As time went by, I became increasingly aware of the paucity of urban facilities for children.

How many green spaces on council estates carry signs saying 'No ball games'? When an urban area becomes run down, how often do we see a suggestion that the area should become a green area, or a place to play? The price and returns on development land are so high that the needs of children rarely even enter the equation. Offices, luxury flats, and new shopping centres are far more rewarding in terms of financial return, but how much more pleasant would our cities be as dwelling places if we allowed nature back to become a regular feature of the urban fabric so that for every square mile of building we insisted on an area of green parkland? It is a travesty for the youth of today that space to play is not a high priority on the agenda of town planners.

Creating an Urban Utopia

A couple of years ago there was a suggestion that the Forestry Commission should be involved in urban projects, looking at ways in which trees and green spaces could be regenerated. It would not take a great deal of imagination to start replanting trees in inner-city areas, helping to oxygenate the environment, improve the water table, encourage bird life back into larger towns, and provide natural playgrounds for the city's children.

As the standard of living for the majority has improved, so the amount of living space per capita has actually decreased. In British Elizabethan times, the meadows and the forest provided a vast playground. William Shakespeare, for example, probably left school at about the age of 14, but his education was far wider than the schoolroom. The countryside and the ever-changing seasons provided food for the senses so that his writing is brimming with colour, the flowers and scents of summer, flavours both bitter and sweet, the climate, and the seasons, all of which provided a palette from which he painted a canvas of emotions and wove stories from keen observation of human nature. Musical composers through the generations have done the same – Schubert's Trout Quintet, Beethoven's Pastoral Symphony – each composer has been attuned to his environment and translated his sensory experiences into a work of art. Rural environments tend to foster increased sensory awareness, while the noisy, busy hustle and bustle of the city teaches us to shut out a plethora of sensory stimuli, unless we allow enough space and time for the senses to breathe.

Children need not only space to play, but also an environment which permits creativity. Whilst playground equipment usually provides plenty of opportunity for vestibular stimulation, imagination tends to be developed in a less ordered environment. A wilderness of long grass, trees, ditches, and stones opens up endless possibilities for games of hide and seek, building a den, being marooned in a jungle, or surviving on a desert island.

In Sweden, where the population density is much lower and there is extensive forestation, the climbing of trees is as natural as using climbing frames in a playground. Yes, there are risks involved, but children learn how to be safe by taking minor risks, making mistakes, and learning how not to make the same mistake again. When I learned to sail, it was said that you were not a sailor until you had capsized. Of course we should keep our children safe, but in order to live with confidence, children also need to learn how to take care of themselves. Part of this is developed through embracing new and challenging experiences – the process of play.

In 2001 the *Times Educational Supplement* started a debate following suggestions that school playtime was dangerous. An increasing tendency for parents to sue following accidents in the school playground had led to suggestions that abolishing playtime was a more attractive proposition, despite evidence which has shown that increased opportunity for physical exercise in the school day is connected to a decrease in incidents of aggression and accidents in the playground.

Between 1992 and 1994 a study was carried out in a Kindergarten in Frankfurt[54] where researchers suspected that accidents in the playground were largely due to lack of body control. A Movement Training programme was introduced for 15 minutes a day; and after just eight weeks, the incidence of accidents had decreased by 50 per cent – and this is by no means an isolated finding. Knowle Primary School in the British Midlands started a 'Fit for Learning' programme[55] in which children were given the opportunity to participate in teacher-led physical play at each break time throughout the day. They noticed a marked reduction in behavioural problems and an increase in attention in the children.

In the thrust for academic achievement, it is often forgotten that in order to pay attention, a child needs to have a degree of control over the body. 'The most advanced level of movement is the ability to stay totally still'[56] – in other words, it is dependent on mature motor skills. The younger the child, the harder it is to sit still for long periods of time. A child who is unable to sit still and maintain attention needs *more* frequent opportunities to move around and to exercise the body in order to concentrate again. By encouraging children to move around at regular intervals through the day, the 'Fit for Learning Project' may have helped children to settle down and concentrate better during lessons, in addition to improving body control. 'Self-control begins with control of the body.'[57]

Education should be a continuous process of sensory as well as intellectual training, not an environment for sensory atrophy (sitting still all day long). Exercise involves three processes that have a powerful impact on learning:

1. Modification of sensory tracts as a result of sensory input;
2. Change in motor areas of the brain and the body, which result directly from initiating new movements and repeating old ones;
3. Modification of *associative* functions of the brain.

Whenever new brain cells are associated, there lies a physical basis for new thoughts and new connections. Memory is also stimulated through action because memory corresponds to definite changes within brain cells, which may be the result of molecular rearrangement or dynamic action. Memory results from *doing* something with sensation.

School Study

I first met Simon when I visited a small church school in the north of England. The school had been using a series of developmental movements, which I had devised, with a whole

137

class every day. The class had been chosen because they were a particularly lively class who were constantly getting into trouble in the playground. Teachers had found the general attention span of the children to be poor, problems in the playground were frequent, and several of the children had been identified as under-achieving in basic academic skills.

All of the children were tested for signs of problems with balance, coordination, retained reflexes, and visual tracking before the programme was started. Drawing ability was also assessed using the 'Draw a Person Test'. The tests were repeated after the equivalent of one academic year, during which time specific developmental movements had been carried out in school for 10 minutes every day during term time under teacher supervision.

The results were remarkable. Children who had previously received high scores on the tests for signs of neurological dysfunction (poor balance coordination, immature reflexes, and visual processing) showed marked improvement at the end. Their drawings were unrecognizable as being the drawings of the same children, such was the increased maturity in representational skills. In many cases, handwriting also showed similar improvement.

When I walked into the school hall that day, I was struck by a boy with close-cropped hair sitting cross-legged in the middle of the hall, eyes closed, calmly doing finger exercises while the rest of the class filed in. Simon was striking because his sitting posture was perfect and because of his stillness. Each child sat down in a similar position and started their own finger exercises until the teacher was ready to work with the whole class. Allegri's 'Miserere' was playing quietly in the background. The children then began a series of slow-motion movements, turning in space and lying on the floor. When the movements became more complicated, a metronome was used to help them to develop an even and flowing rhythm. To a casual observer, the grace of the movements matched those of a ballet dancer, and yet these were the same children who had been rowdy, uncoordinated, and inattentive at the beginning of the school year. I had expected to see changes in reading and writing as a result of improvement in basic motor skills. I was amazed by the changes that had taken place in demeanour, behaviour, and social integration. Each child that I tested showed similar poise, pride, and self-confidence. These children were happy in themselves.

In addition to tests for reading and spelling, all of the children were asked to draw a human figure at the beginning and the end of the programme. As early as the late 1800s, Cooke and Ricci had recognized that children's drawings change over the course of development, and that developmental status can be estimated from the quality and detail contained within children's drawings. In 1921, Burt had noted that developmental progress and delay were evident in children's drawings, and in 1926, Florence Goodenough published her findings that children's drawings relate to intelligence.[58] Since that time, the Draw a Person Test has been used for various purposes, including projective tests for assessment of emotional status.[59]

The children's drawings at the school in Carlisle were assessed using a scoring system devised by Harris in 1963. Harris' scoring system enables the tester to obtain both a mental age and percentile rating score for each child's drawing. The following are illustrated examples of the alteration in children's drawings and perception of their own abilities before and after the movement programme. Table 2 shows the children's neurological scores on tests for balance, reflexes, and visual processing at the beginning and end of the programme, together with the Percentile Rating Score (PRS) on the Draw a Person Test.

A high score on the neurological tests indicates signs of dysfunction.

The PR (percentile rating) score shows the child's score compared to 100 children of the same age, i.e. 99/100 is a high score, 8/100 is eighth from the bottom.

The results show that there was a marked *decrease* in signs of neurological dysfunction after the programme, and that the children's percentile rating *increased* significantly. The teacher also asked the children to write about the changes they had noticed since doing the movements. The children's drawings and letters tell a story far more eloquently than any study, so I have included some of these letters and drawings.

Child 1. 1st Assessment

Child 1. 2nd Assessment

Dear Sally,
You haven't saw me
I was poorly when you wRx were
there here Sory Sally Maby next
time. I the ingants I coulldan't
read. I have in proud with my wrting
because my movement, I Love having
movement. Im concentrated in my
movement. I was good on monday
and I lisnd at scinx Science.

Child 1.

Child 2. 1st Assessment

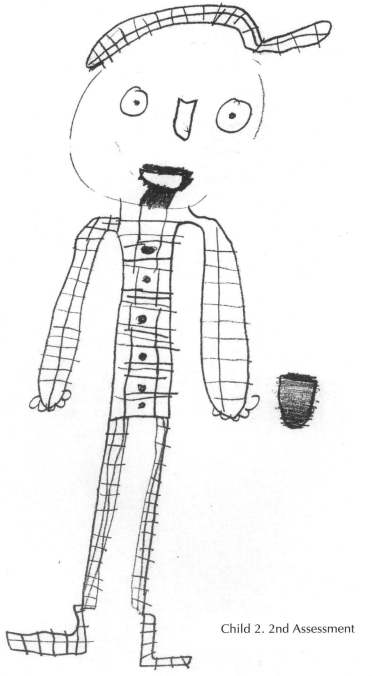

Child 2. 2nd Assessment

Dear Sally,

thankyou for makeing the book becawse it does make me very focused becawse I have got better at every thing. But I have got better at football becawse I can kick etaner and I can keep my head up and focused better in every thing. But I like maths the best and I have got better at puting it in corners.

In the play groud I used to bup in to people but I don't now beca I keep my head up with my neck muser.

On Sataday I am going to play football mach against whitbey Bary and I hope wie will win becawse I am going to be focus on that day and I will keep my head up with my neck meader and everyone will be very happy if we will win and we mignt beat we will I hope. I like doing movement and it is fun.

I like to go into the hall and get
ready and focused and I like
it because I come into the classroom
and I am very focused. But
it makes me work better when I
am focused very well.

Child 2.

Child 3. 1st Assessment

Child 3. 2nd Assessment

Dear Sally,

Your Movement has helped me a lot with My hand writen and in the play ground.

My hand writen use to be arful it's a lot beller now as you can see. the main thing about my hand writen was My neack musels it was hard to prop my neack up.

In the play ground we all use to be bumping into every one and we use to get told of for it, but now when I play rescue I'nnever getting told of now.

Movement is fun and exting every time we do a new movement. Its helped me a lot
          Thank you

Child 3

Child 4. 1st Assessment

a young man

Child 4.
2nd
Assessment

Dear Sally,

Before I started movement I was hopeless at forming letters I still have room to improve, but on the whole I'm better than I used to be. I love to write but it's a bit of a problem because I feel that my writing is scrunched up, movement has really helped me because my hands no longer ache. However I believe I have definately become a better listener in my maths I used to switch off when big numbers or decimals came up but movement helped me concentrate and focus. I play netball and and the finger tracking helped my hand - eye co- ordination.

My whole class had a problem with this - the playground d we were always running and flinging our arms out at the same, this caused lots of problems and accidents we banged into people almost every day, then movement began and we went into small spaces and kept our head up and arms in we used our shoulders to dodge, now we don't get into trouble for that.
It's really fun and now I feel confident and proud!
Me and my class really appreciate it.

Child 4

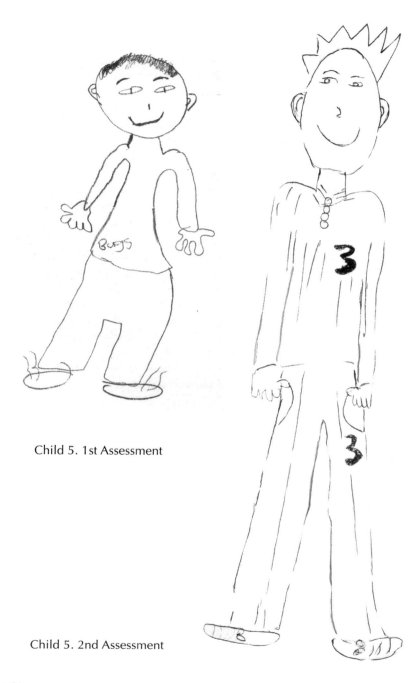

Child 5. 1st Assessment

Child 5. 2nd Assessment

Dear Sally,

Thank you for coming over to see us do our movement. I have noticed that I have got better at my dancing, running and swimming by doing movement. I can remember when I use to do my writing I use to put my head on the table but now I don't because my breck muscles hold my head up. When we have to listen to the teacher I have noticed that I use my eye contact and when we done quite read in year four I can remember I use to lose my place and I read the whole page again, and I have noticed my handwriting has got better and when it was playtime we use to all bang into each other. ~~but~~ Now we don't because our movement has helped us alot. I have noticed that I concentrate and focus more in class now. ~~and~~ My breck muscles and shoulder muscle use to always ache but I have really got on with my movement, it has really helped me and I feel condife ~~and~~ I am proued of myself as well.

Child 5

Child 6. 1st Assessment

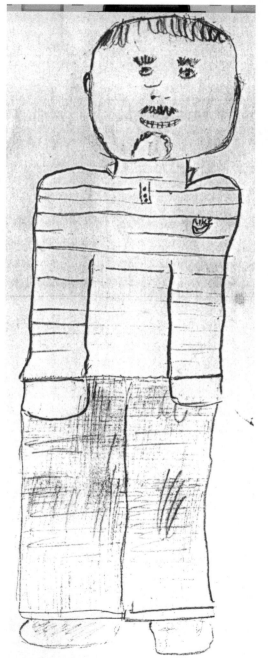

Child 6. 2nd Assessment

Dear Sally,
thankyou for coming I really appreciate it. My movement has really helped me consentrate and get on with my handwritting it has also helped mey horseriding In class movement has helped me to focus more Now I listen more because I consentrate. In handwritting I used to find writting letters very hard but now I don't. I think in my body that it all works very well together now my hands don't ache when I write. I feel proud of my self now because my handwritting is much bell better. In the playground i always used to get into trouble but now I streamline my self.

Child 6

Child 7. 1st Assessment

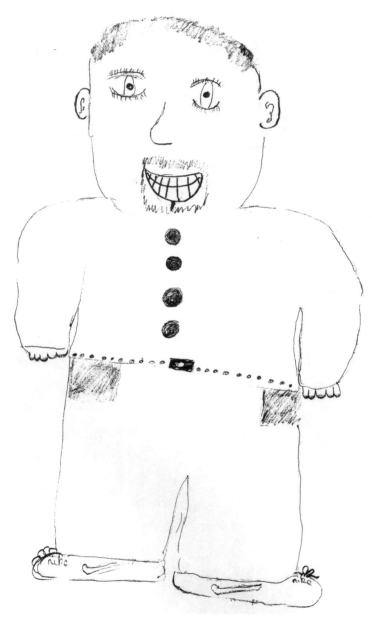

Child 7. 2nd Assessment

Dear Sally,

Thank you for all your help. you helped me be more focesed. In year four I was really bad at consentrating and my handwriting whex went on a slope Now when I write it stays strate and my hand doesen't get saw.

At the start of year five I allways got into trubbel for bumping into peopel but now I can just swerve away for people and it is all because of my mavment. Now my mucels are stonger and I feel a lot better.

Child 7

Child 8. 1st Assessment

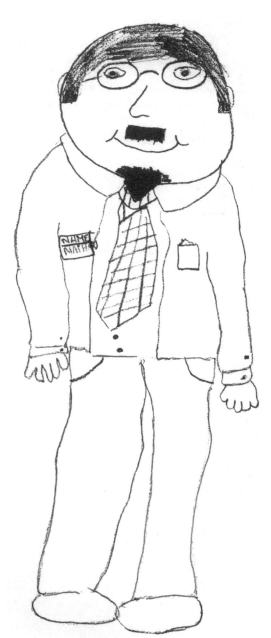

Child 8. 2nd Assessment

Dear Sally

Thank you for comming to our School. Since you came we have all done better doing the cat, commando crawl and the croadiale crawl. Before you came I could'nt write neat or concentrate, So thank you for helping us. I'm Still not Sure about the cat. It's the bit when we rock back and fourth because I get muddled up when we have to rock forwod then count to five. It's just I keep forgetting to go foward. Anyway thank you for comming we all had a great time I hope you come again.

bye
for
now

Child 8

Child 9. 1st
Assessment

Child 9. 2nd Assessment

Dear
Sally

Before I , started Movement I was all
-Ways bumping into people and getting in
trouble. Then I found Handwriting berouse
I use to put my, head on the table
but now I consantate now I learn not to
put my head on the table. I like the
way you do movement. It is fun
the way you do movement.

The way We do it now is xeelent
I can controll my body NOW. I
can run faster An I can write
better now.

Child 9

Child 10.
1st Assessment

Child 10.
2nd Assessment

Dear Sally,
    Ever since you have wrote those books, my life has changed. I have written load's of storys, even my mam has been saying you must of been a great writter, because you have helped me and my class. I didnt like this subject because my hands use to ache, hurt and sting with pain. You have helped me alot thankyou for everything

Child 10

Table 2
Change in Neurological Scores and Percentile Rating Score on the Draw a Person Test before and after nine months of Developmental Exercises in School

Child	Neurological 1st Assessment	PR Score for Drawing 1st Assessment	Neurological 2nd Assessment	PR Score for Drawing 2nd Assessment
1	17/40	1	2.5/40	68
2	28/40	8	4/40	68
3	19/40	1	2.5/40	39
4	12.5/40	91	1/40	98
5	21/40	73	1.5/40	90
6	15.5/40	39	0.5/40	53
7	25.5/40	82	1/40	95
8	24/40	90	2,5/40	99
9	23/40	68	0/40	92
10	22/40	37	1/40	84

Simon played in a local football team along with several members of his class. Although they were playing a middle school (older children), out of four matches they won three and drew one. Simon was so determined that he won the 'Man of the Match' Award.

Maturity in the functioning of the Central Nervous System is reflected in neurological development. Immaturity in the functioning of the Central Nervous System can affect children's sensory-motor abilities and therefore the way that they perceive space, objects in space including body image, and their attention to detail etc. These children's drawings are remarkable for the changes that occurred following the movement programme in their use of space on the page, detail contained within the drawings, and position in relation to gravity. Whilst some of the children still had problems at the end of the programme, *all* had made significant progress both in neurological status and maturity in the drawing of a human figure.

The class teacher also commented on changes noticed by all members of staff in the school:

'There is a dignity to these children that was never there before. They no longer bump into each other in the playground, which they used to do all the time, and they are far more considerate towards each other. They enjoy doing the movements, have a pride in themselves and are far calmer and more focused for the morning classes having done their exercises at the start of the day. As their confidence and self-control have increased they have started to have ambitions for the future. One child who had severe coordination problems at the beginning of the programme said he wanted to be a teacher of coordination when he grows up. Many of these children had never had ambition beyond wanting to reach the end of the lesson before.'[60]

The movements used at this school were highly specific developmental movements based on the Reflex Stimulation and Inhibition Programmes devised at the Institute for Neuro-Physiological Psychology, Chester, UK since the 1970s.[61] The Developmental Programme used by the school in Carlisle, UK is being used by a number of schools in the United Kingdom, Germany, Ireland, and the United States. Early pilot projects have shown significant improvement in reading, writing, drawing, and spelling of children who have taken part in the projects, and more formal studies are now underway. The first follow-up study to be carried out three years after finishing the programme suggests that gains made while doing the programme are maintained over time.[62]

The programme outlined above is only one type of movement programme. There are, of course, many others which have also been shown to be effective in improving coordination and enhancing other aspects of learning.

10. Learning from the Ancients: Education through Movement

'Modern education is conducted much on the same method as geese are fattened for the market. In the one case, so much food is thrust down the throat, in the other, so much knowledge is forced into the brain. Whether it is properly assimilated is a matter of small concern.'

Men Only Magazine, February 1941

All of life is about adaptation and change, and as long as we are able to adapt to the demands of our environment we can survive. However, sometimes in the process of change, in our hurry to embrace new ideas and new inventions, we ignore the value of traditions and customs that have grown up as a result of generations of accumulated wisdom. In our enthusiasm to follow what is new, we are sometimes too ready to discard the old, only to discover much later that something of infinite value has been lost. The role of movement and music in education has been a central theme of this book. This is not a new concept, but rather a revival of traditions that were central to education for over 2,000 years and which have only relatively recently been relegated to the back shelf.

In primitive societies most learning takes place as a result of simple, unconscious imitation. The first priority is to meet the practical needs of the environment – learning how to build and maintain a shelter, hunt, fish, skin an animal, and generally learn the skills that support survival. The second level of training is in the forms of worship and customs of the group, which collectively enable a group of people to live together in a society. These rituals or laws by which individual peoples live are learned through imitation and experience.

Oriental Education

'What heaven has conferred is called nature; an accordance with nature is called the path of duty; the regulation of this path is called instruction.'

Confucian text

The purpose of education in the ancient Orient was to train each individual in the path of duty; within this path, minute details of life's occupations and relationships were laid down. Some of Confucian philosophy was reinforced by the two other religions of China, Buddhism and Taoism, in which all ethical teaching and social obligations were contained within the 'five relationships' of sovereign and subject, parent and child, husband and wife, brother and brother, friend and friend. These were taught to every child in ten syllables as the A,B,C of social conduct – a Ten Commandments of the East. In this way, the philosophy of life and society formed the basis for education, and education supported the stability of the state and society.

In both Oriental and Greek education, one of the aims was to achieve a balance between excess and denial. Moderation in all things was a virtue – "a doctrine of the mean". Whilst education for boys was carried out in an institution, in the East it was the family who provided the *basis* for education, because the family contained all the ingredients for the practice of the five relationships, which were the foundation of the sacred texts.

The aim of elementary education was to instruct a boy in the language and literature of the sacred texts. Chinese is an ideographic, not a phonetic language in which characters represent ideas, not sounds. Meaning is given to the eye rather than the ear. Unlike the 26 characters of Arabic script, there are an infinite number of characters in Chinese in which any change of meaning is denoted by a stress mark, either in the way the character is written or by the position of stress in the voice.

Early education was devoted to the memorizing of the characters contained in sacred texts, followed by translation, and eventually the writing of essays. Early teaching was based purely on precise imitation – the training of memory. Each child would take a section of text and 'shout aloud' the passage until it was remembered and could be repeated correctly. At the end of the day, he would be required to 'back his book', which involved handing his book to the teacher, turning his back on the teacher, and reciting the passage at full speed without necessarily any understanding of the meaning of the text. Vocal repetition helped to develop memory.

Writing was also taught through simple imitation. Because of the minute differences in meaning between characters, accuracy in writing was crucial, so the formation of characters was learned first with tracing paper, then using a brush, and finally a pen. In this way, a *kinaesthetic* memory for how characters should be formed was developed, sometimes in advance of understanding. By the time a child passed from elementary to the next level of education, both memory and the movement patterns needed for the formation of characters were highly developed skills.

Arithmetic did not appear as a separate discipline at all but was learned through experience; the handling of cash, purchases, and so on. If more advanced mathematical skills were required, these were learned through practice from an expert in the field – a kind of apprenticeship. In this way, most Chinese education was still based upon imitation.

Criticism of the Oriental style of education in later years was based on the fact that emphasis on imitation alone does not train both sides of the brain. It develops an excellent memory, mastery of detail, and discrimination of form, but it does not encourage the development of initiative, creativity, or adaptability. In this respect, it is the perfect education for a society that has no desire to change. It was primarily an education of recapitulation.

Greek Education

Greek education still required obedience to the State, but within this code of obedience there was room for change and development of the individual. Individuals found their freedom through the State, and freedom was obtained through the love of knowledge, enquiry into nature, the origin of the universe and the state of man, expressed by Socrates as the duty of every individual 'to know himself'. It was through the realization of his own nature that man must solve the problems of the universe, so that science, art, religion, and philosophy were simply a means to greater understanding of life and all the processes of living – a search for truth. Greek education aimed to realize the development of the individual *through* the institutions of State.

Unlike Oriental education, Greek education was highly practical. It was based on action first, followed by learning. Boys started school at the age of 7 when they would learn to run races, to jump, and to wrestle. The aims of Greek education were contained within 'the twofold ideal' – the man of wisdom personified by Odysseus, and the man of action typified by Achilles. To this end, the State required training in *music* and

167

gymnastics. Plato[63] described the function of these two branches of education:

> 'The teachers of the lyre take similar care that their young disciples are temperate and get into no mischief; and when they have taught them the use of the lyre, they introduce them to poems and poems set to music. These poems set to music make their harmonies and rhythms quite familiar to the children's souls, in order that they may learn to be more gentle and harmonious, and rhythmical, and so more fitted for speech and action; for the life of man in every part has need for harmony and rhythm. They then send him to the master of gymnastic, in order that their bodies may better minister to the virtuous mind, and that they may not be compelled through bodily weakness to play the coward in war or on any other occasion.'

The two main elements of education, 'gymnastic for the body, music for the soul', helped to develop whole-mindedness or temperance: control of passion and command of reason. Mastery of aggression was achieved through strength. Music provided the gateway to poetry, drama, history, oratory, and science. Herodotus and Thucydides laid the foundations of science, but it began as an art form – the writing of history. Even today the young undergraduate reading History is often asked to define whether the study of History is an Art or a Science.

Physical education placed emphasis on the proper form of exercise. Grace and dignified carriage, control of temper, and skill were far more highly prized than winning.

Small children played a whole series of games in the home in the years before starting school, starting with ball games which led into contests of running and other simple forms of exercises known as callisthenics. At school these were organized into a more formal arrangement, the Pentathlon, which included jumping, running, throwing the discus, throwing the spear, and wrestling. Discus throwing and javelin casting provided excellent arm exercise and helped to develop poise, timing, and symmetry. Javelin throwing developed precision of hand/eye coordination. Many varieties of wrestling were taught, which required agility, concentration of energy, endurance, speed, inventiveness, and control of temper. Wrestling later developed into boxing with open palms of the hands.

Dancing was also important, and was not confined to the development of social skills. Dancing was performed in civic processions, military drill, and religious rites. Dancing provided training for harmonious action with others (something we might take note of today, when much modern dancing is an isolated activity in which the dancers on the floor 'do their own thing' and the only unity between dancers is the unremitting pulse or beat of the music). The training of both music and gymnastics found unity in the dance – the unity of harmony, physical development, and emotional experience.

Plato produced an outline for the education of children and youth. Formal education began at age 7, and continued up to 16 or 17 in the study of Gymnastics and Music. Gymnastics was to develop harmony of the body (the word 'aesthete' originally meant athlete) and Music for harmony of the soul. Music was the chief means of moral education. Subjects such as reading, writing, and arithmetic were not taught as formal disciplines but were introduced as occasional activities as the study of scientific form underlying the Arts. Many centuries later, Christian monasticism owed much of its way of life to a blend of a Platonic philosophy and Oriental aestheticism.

The Roman Way

After the Roman conquest in 146 BC, the Romans appropriated much of Greek culture and education. Whereas the Greeks believed that beauty, grace, and moral fibre are assimilated through works of art, social etiquette, and so on, the Romans believed in imitation from a model – a more concrete style of learning. Gymnastics, dancing, music, and literature were rejected as being effeminate, but the training of physical development was continued through military training. All forms of training for boys were accomplished through apprenticeship, learning from a master by doing, whether the Master was a soldier, a farmer, or a future statesman. Education was through the father (for boys) and a Master, combined with education in the art of citizenship. It was once again an education through action, although the rudiments of reading, writing, and arithmetic were also taught.

Music was not an integral part of education as it had been in the Greek sense, but it was an important part of social life – state occasions, entertainment, and great banquets. Musicians had an honoured place in their own right, but street entertainers who used a mixture of acrobatics (tumblers), juggling, and music were also a feature of Roman life. The street entertainers of Roman times were the forerunners of the medieval minstrels or jongleurs who were, in turn, the predecessor of modern circus entertainers.

With the decline and fall of the Roman Empire, it was left to the Christian church to draw into itself the knowledge of the Greek and Roman cultures. But in its reaction against the corrupt society of its pagan forbears, the Christian church tended to pay less attention to the intellectual aspects of learning, and to concentrate its energies instead on the moral aspects of education and reform. Despite this, the church remained the most constant force in the Western world to continue education through the Dark Ages to the Renaissance.

The study of Greek philosophy was suppressed by the Eastern Church, which considered the influences of Gnosticism and Neoplatonism to be heretical. These might well have been lost for ever, had it not been for the Saracen who preserved much of this knowledge, passing it from the Syrians to a Christian sect in Western Asia – the Nestorians – where texts were translated from Greek or Syrian into Arabic. Mathematics, the natural sciences, and the basis for medical science were fostered here and later passed to the School of Cordova in Spain:

> 'Between the middle of the eighth and the thirteenth centuries, the Arabic speaking peoples were the main bearers of the torch of culture and civilisation throughout the world. Moreover they were the medium through which ancient science and philosophy were recovered, supplemented and transmitted in such a way as to make possible the renaissance of Western Europe.'[64]

From the Arabs of the tenth and eleventh centuries comes our modern knowledge of algebra, pharmacy, physiology, and astronomy. They explained the refraction of light and gravity; they invented the pendulum clock, and after the Chinese, the use of a compass, gunpowder, and cannon. While the Western church insisted that the world was flat, the Moors were teaching geography from globes.

The Western Church did, however, nurture the song schools and the monastic schools where the ideal of asceticism – the training and disciplining of the athlete for physical contests – was redirected into the subjugation of bodily desires in the pursuit of a higher life. Many of the rituals of worship link the use of the body to the higher aspirations of the soul. Processions at festival time, genuflection, kneeling, and standing at important moments in the service, use change of body position to remind the flock of the meaning of the moment.

The Age of Chivalry

In secular life, the age of chivalry continued some of the Roman traditions of education through imitation and preparation for military life. Chivalry encompassed a set of high social ideals that were realized through established customs and sanctioned by the Church. The aspiring knight served his pupillage as a page from about the age of 7, for a period of seven years. During this time the page would become part of an organized household or court where he would be expected to wait upon table, care for the horses, and help maintain the stable and the bedchamber. The emphasis was on the duty of service. At about the age of 14, the page would become a squire who continued his duties, but also became accomplished in the arts of love, war, and religion. The rudiments of love were learned by attendance on the ladies and from the teaching of the minstrels.

The young squire might also learn to play the harp and to sing. These were the gentle qualities. The rudiments of war were acquired through physical training – riding, learning to use a sword, lance and javelin, and in hunting. Physical training through medieval 'sports' developed physical strength and endurance. There was little of literature in the training of the young knight, save the requirement to understand French (the language of chivalry) and the learning of song from the minstrels. In the age of chivalry, physical education and music were still key elements of education.

Some 500 years later, in Germany, Friedrich Froebel developed a philosophy of education based partly on the ideas of Rousseau, who had advocated the need to return to nature (education must allow the natural goodness in the child to unfold) and Pestalozzi. Pestalozzi believed that education should entail 'the harmonious development of all powers of the individual'. Froebel embraced the natural active nature of learning, and saw play as the educational method whereby the child's inner powers could be released. His pre-school curriculum focused on the developmental needs of the child and was provided within a framework of 'gifts and occupations', songs, games, and movement activities.

Some years later, Margaret and Rachel McMillan, considered by many to be the founders of the nursery-school movement, set up a school clinic for the treatment of ailments in school-aged children. Margaret McMillan strongly believed that medical inspection of school children was essential to the creation of a healthy nation. Children under 5 were also welcomed to the clinic, as both the McMillan sisters became convinced that prevention of ailment and disability was as important as the treatment of existing conditions. From this belief, the concept of an 'open air nursery' grew. The McMillans, like John Locke, believed that a healthy mind needed a healthy body. Margaret wrote,

'Children want space at all ages, but from age one to seven, that is ample space, wanted almost as much as food and air. To move, to run, to find things out by new movement, to feel one's life in every limb, that is the life of early childhood. And yet one sees dim houses behind whose windows and doors thirty or forty little ones are penned in Day Nurseries. Bare sites and open spaces are what we need today.'[65]

She went on to say, 'the open air Nursery School is here for rich and poor. It is here, the thing lacking – our whole educational system was like a house built on the sand.'

Kindergarten and Nursery School Provision

Whilst the McMillan sisters were setting up their open air nurseries, Maria Montessori built upon the principles of Froebel, by placing emphasis on thorough and scientific training in sensory discrimination. Sensory training could be accomplished through a combination of special exercises, through play and through activities and occupations, which naturally occur in the daily life of the child. Although the concept of freedom was important, this did not imply freedom without responsibility. Montessori advocated the provision of full opportunity for the exercise and expression of the child's motor activities, provided they were not anti-social, and teaching the tempering of anti-social behaviour and conflict by helping the child to develop self-regulation of its own behaviour through teacher guidance, direction, and inspiration.

Hence, the Montessori schools were not only responsible for instruction, but also the teaching of life skills. Children were taught to wash themselves, brush their teeth, and generally keep things tidy. During a full school day, lunch was provided and the children had to learn how to lay and clear the tables, to observe table manners, and to wash up. Learning began with experience, and the role of the teacher was to suggest rather than to command.

In a similar vein, education based on the theories of Rudolf Steiner recognizes that 'at each developmental stage, a child presents a particular set of physical, emotional and intellectual characteristics, which require a particular educational response in return'.[66] The onset of secondary dentition is seen as a landmark in terms of 'learning readiness'. Until the shedding of the milk teeth, energy is primarily devoted to physical growth and development. During these years a child's primary mode of learning should be through activity and experience. Sometime during the seventh year the child becomes ready for formal instruction, although this time can vary considerably between children; and in children with neuro-developmental issues the time of readiness for formal education may be delayed even longer. Steiner education 'encourages children to master physical skills before abstract intellectual ones'.[67] In the early years, learning is acquired through 'doing' and 'being', and the formal skills and disciplines of literacy and numeracy are built upon the basis of experiential learning.

Many of these concepts have been incorporated into modern nursery provision, but with each new generation a message can become diluted. Often these days, we play lip-service to the importance of play, but fail to provide the space, the time, or the conditions in which free physical play can take place. Ray Barsch[68] described the young child as a 'terranaut' – a traveller in space who must learn to control the body on terra firma, if he is to become secure in a gravity-based environment and 'make sense' of the world around him. Learning, like balance, begins in space.

Summary

The early years of life provide a foundation for all later learning. Karl Lange believed that the knowledge a child acquires by 6 years of age surpasses anything that he may learn at university. This is partly due to the fact that the plasticity of nerve cells is inversely proportional to their age. Long before the dawn of modern neurology, the Jesuits at the time of the Counter-Reformation had realized that if they could influence a child before the age of 7 years, then that influence would remain with the individual for life. A.A. Milne summed up the importance of being 6, when he said, 'Now I am six I am as clever as clever, and I think I will stay six for ever and ever'! There is a certain element of truth in this particular desire, because an adult is largely the result of the many nerve reactions that he acquired in youth, which tend to express and perpetuate themselves based on early experience.

Whilst the above is a highly selected view of aspects of education in history, it is nevertheless a reminder of the importance of physical development for the training of the mind. The relationship between the brain and mind has been the subject of centuries of debate. To me, the mind is the product of the relationship between the brain and the body, neurologically, chemically, and developmentally. The mind is the result of the history of development of the individual, and if the brain is separated from the body, the mind quickly ceases to exist.

Conclusion

Education means 'to lead people out' – in other words, to nurture and develop the latent abilities of the individual, to introduce them to the possibilities of the world around them, afford them the opportunity of building upon the wisdom and structures of the past, and to develop skills and disciplines that will enable them to seek out new knowledge in the future.

When we teach the body we also nourish the brain, not only in terms of strengthening and maintaining neural connections, but also in refining the chemical and hormonal status of the brain, which collectively contributes to the psyche or the self. For although in modern times we sometimes hear the brain likened to a computer, it is far more than this. It also operates on a complex cocktail of chemicals and physical sources of energy, which are ever-changing in response to the internal and external environment of the individual. If we attempt to feed the brain (through cognitive education) or the body alone, we do not create a 'well balanced' child.

Effective education teaches all levels and systems in the brain through a combination of instruction and physical development. When instruction is matched to the developmental capabilities of the child, we can see the opening of an enquiring mind that is able to approach the world with confidence and seek out the answers to the questions and conundrums of life, which alter in subtle ways with the changing perspectives of every generation. If the demands of the environment exceed the developmental capabilities of the child, the child quickly learns frustration and failure, and may subsequently develop inappropriate coping strategies and defence mechanisms.

The evolution of child development is a gradual process, which takes much longer than changes of attitude and policy in education. Development is the constant factor that remains stable through shifting fads and fashions.

Surely then, it is human development which provides the key to understanding the basis of how our children learn.

General Themes in Child Development

- Life is synonymous with movement.
- Sensory-motor functioning reveals an individual's experience of movement.
- Movement opportunity helps to develop motor performance.
- Motor skills are involved in all aspects of expressive language.
- Sensory-motor skills operate along a continuous feedback loop; refinement of sensory processing will often improve related motor skills, and practice of motor skills can further refine sensory processing.
- Language begins as a body-based function. Change in emotional status can be seen in alteration of posture, gesture, speed, and fluency of movement.
- Speech is a multi-sensory and motor skill involving the

translation of visual images and emotional experience into different elements of sound: pitch, tone, rhythm, phrasing, timing, and cadence. These, together with the fine muscle control required for the use of the lips, tongue, swallow mechanism, and breathing, form the non-verbal aspects of speech, which are important to convey meaning and intent.

- Music naturally contains all of the 'sound' elements of speech and is a form of language without words.
- The process of singing or chanting unites the dual aspects of speech.
- Food provides fuel for growth, energy, cell repair, hormonal balance, and how nerve cells communicate with each other (via neurotransmitters). Energy obtained from food is pumped into the system more efficiently when we move. The quality, variety, and timing of food intake can have a major impact, not only on the physical status of the body but also cognitive processes, mood, and impulse control.
- Routines and social practices help to create bonds between individuals, knitting the child into the social fabric of her environment and helping to form the basis for meaningful relationships.

Whilst so much energy is focused on succeeding at the higher aspects of learning, we should never forget that it is the foundations that make a house stable. The same is true for the Well Balanced Child.

Acknowledgement

I am indebted to Paul Monroe whose excellent book *A Textbook in the History of Education* (1914) was a major source of inspiration and information for the writing of this chapter.

Footnotes

1. W. Oosterveldt, 'The development of the vestibular system', 3rd European Conference of Neuro-Developmental Delay in Children with Specific Learning Difficulties, Chester, UK, 1991.

2. D. Bainbridge, *A Visitor Within: The Science of Pregnancy*, Weidenfeld and Nicolson, London, 2000.

3. O. Schrager, 'Posture and balance: important markers for children's learning development', 13th European Conference of Neuro-Developmental Delay in Children with Specific Learning Difficulties, Chester, UK, 2001.

4. P. Blythe and D. J. McGlown, *An Organic Basis for Neuroses and Educational Difficulties*, Insight Publications, Chester, 1979.

5. H. L. Levinson, *Smart but Feeling Dumb*, Warner Books Inc., New York, 1984; J. B. DeQuiros and O. Schrager, *Neurophysiological Fundamentals in Learning Disabilities*, Academic Therapy Publications, Nevato, Calif., 1978; R. Kohen-Raz, *Learning Disabilities and Postural Control*, Freund Publishing House, London, 1986.

6. D. L. Clarke and others, 'Vestibular stimulation influence on motor development in infants', *Science*, **196**, 1977, pp. 1228-9.

7. S. A. Goddard, *A Teacher's Window into the Child's Mind*, Fern Ridge Press, Eugene, Oreg., 1996.

8. P. Blythe, *Somatogenic Neuroses and the Effect upon Health*, Institute for Psychosomatic Medicine, Chester, 1974.

9. A. Gesell, *The Embryology of Behavior*, Mac Keith Press, London, 1945 and 1988.

10. K. R. Rosenberg and W. R. Trevathen, *The Evolution of Human Birth*, *Scientific American* Special Edition, 2003.

11. W. DeMyer, *Techniques of the Neurological Examination*, McGraw-Hill, New York, 1980.

12. A. Gesell, op cit. (note 9).

13. T. Fukuda, 'Studies on human dynamic postures from the viewpoint of postural reflexes', *Acta. Oto-Laryng.*, suppl. **161**, 1961

14. S. A. Goddard Blythe, 'Neurological dysfunction as a significant underlying factor in children diagnosed with Dyslexia', Paper presented at the 5th International British Dyslexia Association Conference, University of York, April 2001.

15. W. Bein-Wierzbinski, 'Persistent primitive reflexes in elementary school children: effect on oculo-motor and visual perception', Paper presented at the 13th European Conference of Neuro-Developmental Delay in Children with Specific Learning Difficulties, Chester, UK, 2001.

16. J. M. Allman, *Evolving Brains*, Scientific American Library, New York, 2000.

17. Ködding, *Mschr. Kinderlik.*, 842, 1940, p. 212.

18. A. Peiper, *Cerebral Function in Infancy and Early Childhood*, International Behavioral Sciences Series, New York, 1963.

19. O. L. Schrager, 'Posture and balance: important markers for children's learning development', Paper presented at the 13th European Conference of Neuro-Developmental Delay in Children with Specific Learning Difficulties, Chester, UK, 2001.

20. V. Dickson, Personal communication, 1990.

21. S.A. Goddard, *Reflexes, Learning and Behavior*, Fern Ridge Press, Eugene, Oreg., 2002.

22. L. J. Beuret, 'The role of postural reflexes in learning, part 2', Paper presented to the 12th European Conference of Neuro-Developmental Delay in Children with Specific Learning Difficulties, Chester, UK, 2000.

23. R. P. Halleck, *Education of the Nervous System*, Macmillan and Company Ltd., New York, 1898.

24. R. Fisher, Voice trials, held for choristers, Chester, UK, 1993.

25. P. Madaule, Listening Workshop Seminar (sponsored by INPP), Chester, UK, November 2001.

26. J. Barwick, cited in *Brain Mind Bulletin*, March 1990: 'Observed tie between music, reading may stem from elements in common', *Journal of Educational Psychology*, **59**, 1990

27. B. Lloyd, Supervision Seminar, arranged by the Institute for Neuro-Physiological Psychology, Chester, UK, 1994.

28. Y.-C. Ho, M.-C. Cheung, and A. S. Chan, 'Music training improves verbal but not visual memory: cross sectional and longitudinal explorations in children', *Neuropsychology*, **17** (3), 2003, pp. 439-50.

29. K. R. Pelletier, cited in H. Smith and T. Moore (eds), *Gregorian Chant: Songs of the Spirit*, KQED Books, San Francisco, 1996.

30. P. Madaule, The Ear Voice Connection Workshop, Seminar, Chester, November.

31. A. Schore, *Affect Regulation and the Origin of the Self*, Laurence Erlbaum Associates, Hove, UK, 1994.

32. R. Fisher, Personal communication, 2003.

33. K. Le Mée, *Chant*, Random House, London, 1994.

34. R. Fisher, Personal communication, 2003.

35. J. Leeds, *Sonic Alchemy*, Inner Song Press, Sausalito, Calif., 1997.

36. K. Gardner, *Sounding the Inner Landscape: Music as Medicine*, Element, Rockport, Mass., 1990.

37. J. Leeds, op. cit.

38. H. C. Leiner, A. L. Leiner, and R. S. Dow, 'Does the cerebellum contribute to mental skills?', *Behavioral Neuroscience*, 100, 1986, pp. 443-54.

39. D. Barker, cited in J. M. Nash, 'Inside the womb', *Time Magazine*, 18th November, 2002.

40. A. Richardson, 'Fatty acids in Dyslexia, Dyspraxia, ADHD and the Autistic spectrum', *Nutrition Practitioner*, 3 (3), 2001, pp. 18 –24.

41. S. B. Edleson, Internet Information available from Edelson Centre for Environmental and Preventive Medicine, 3833, Roswell Rd, Suite 110, Atlanta,.Ga. 30342, 1995, *emphasis added*.

42. B. Barnes, *A Layperson's Notes on the Interpretation of Mineral Analysis*, Foresight Publications, Godalming, Surrey, no date (booklet).

43. D. F. Caldwell, D. Oberleas, and A. S. Prasad, *Psychobiological Changes in Zinc Deficiency*, Trace Elements in Human Health and Disease 1, Academic Press, London, 1976.

44. D. Bryce-Smith and L. Hodgkinson, *The Zinc Solution*, Century Arrow, London, 1986.

45. B. Barnes, Personal communications, 1990, 1991.

46. Ibid.

47. K. Eaton, Paper presented at the 11th European Conference of Neuro-Developmental Delay in Children with Specific Learning Difficulties, Chester, 1999.

48. N. G. Jablonski and G. Chaplin, *Skin Deep*, Scientific American Special Edition, 2003.

49. E. Weatherhead (1996), cited in Jablonski and Chaplin, ibid.

50. A. J. Riopelle and D. C. Hubbard, 'Prenatal manganese deprivation and early behaviour of primates', *Journal of Ortho-Molecular Psychiatry*, 6, 1977, pp. 327-33.

51. C. P. W. Bennett, *Writings on Nutrition and Behaviour*, Restorative Health Company, Ottery St Mary, Devon, 2002.

52. H. Pettman, *The Effect of Developmental Exercise Movements on Children with Persistent Primary Reflexes and Reading Difficulties: A Controlled Trial*, Department of Education and Skills, London, Best Practice Research Scholarship, 2000; S. Bertram (2002), *The Prince Albert School Pilot Study*, cited in S. A. Goddard Blythe, 'Neurological dysfunction, a developmental exercise programme used in schools and the effect upon learning', Paper presented at the Bangor Dyslexia Conference, Bangor, North Wales, July 2003.

53. J. Panksepp, *Affective Neuroscience*, Oxford University Press, Oxford, 1998.

54. Frankfurt Kindergarten Study, cited in E. J. Kiphard, 'Intervention programmes using the German psycho-motor approach with exceptional children', Paper presented at the 12th European Conference of Neuro-Developmental Delay in Children with Specific Learning Difficulties, Chester, UK, 2000.

55. P. Preedy, 'Fit for Learning' Programme, Knowle Primary School, Solihull, 2001-2003.

56. N. Rowe, Personal communication, 1994-5.

57. Kiphard, op. cit. (note 54).

58. J. A. Naglieri, DAP Draw a Person Test: A Quantitative Scoring System Manual, Psychological Corporation, Harcourt Brace-Javonovic Inc., San Antonio, 1988.

59. K. Machover, *Personality Projection in the Drawing of the Human Figure*, Charles C. Thomas. Springfield, Ill., 1949.

60. E. Sylvester, The Carlisle Project, personal communication, 2002.

61. P. Blythe and D. J. McGlown, *An Organic Basis for Neuroses and Educational Difficulties*, Insight Publications, Chester, UK, 1979; P. Blythe, Exercises developed at INPP, Chester,

1982-96; S. A. Goddard Blythe, *Developmental Test Battery and Exercise Programme for use in Schools with Children with Specific Learning Difficulties and/or Coordination Problems*, Institute for Neuro-Physiological Psychology, Chester, UK, 1996.

62. M. Jändling, 'The use of the INPP movement programme at a German primary school', Paper presented at the 15th European Conference of Neuro-Developmental Delay in Children with Specific Learning Difficulties, Kiel-Oslo-Kiel, 2003.

63. Plato, cited in Jowett, *The Protagoras*. Trans. Vol. 1.

64. P. K. Hitti, *History of the Arabs*, Macmillan Press, London, 1977.

65. Cited in S. J. Curtis, *History of Education in Great Britain*, University Tutorial Press Ltd., London, 1950, p. 333.

66. M. Rawson and T. Richter T, *The Educational Tasks and Content of the Steiner Waldorf Curriculum*, Steiner School Fellowship Publications, Forest Row, Sussex, 2000.

67. Ibid.

68. Ray H. Barsch, 'Achieving perceptual-motor efficiency. A space-oriented approach to learning', *Perceptual-Motor Curriculum*, Vol. 1, 1968.

General References

Alexander, D. (2002) Personal Communication

Al-Ghazali (1111), *quoted in* Giladi, A. (1992) *Children of Islam: Concepts of Childhood in Medieval Muslim Society*, McMillan, Basingstoke

Ayres, A. J. (1979/1982) *Sensory Integration and the Child*, Western Psychological Services, Los Angeles, Calif.

Bender, M. L. (1976) *Bender-Purdue Reflex Test*, Academic Publications, San Rafael, Calif.

Blythe, P. and McGlown, D. J. (1979) *An Organic Basis for Neuroses and Educational Difficulties*, Insight Publications, Chester

Boethius, A. (Sixth Century)

Burt, C. (1921) *Mental and Scholastic Tests*, P. S. King & Son, London

Cooke and Ricci (1800s), cited in Naglieri, J. A. (1988) *DAP Draw a Person: A Quantitative Scoring System*, The Psychological Corporation, Harcourt Brace Jovanovich, Inc., New York

Crawford, M. (1994) *cited in* Morgan, E. (1994) *The Descent of the Child*, Souvenir Press, London

Eaton, K. (1999) Paper presented at the 11th European Conference of Neuro-Developmental Delay in Children with Specific Learning Difficulties, Chester

Edwards, B. (1989) *Drawing on the Right Side of the Brain*, Souvenir Press, UK

Froebel, F. (1899) *Education by Development*, New York

Froebel, F. (1902) *Pedagogics of the Kindergarten*, New York

Fukuda, T. (1961) 'Studies on human dynamic postures from the viewpoint of postural reflexes', *Acta. Oto-Laryng.*, suppl. 161

Galant, S. (1917) *Der Rückgratreflex*, Diss, Basel

Gesell, A. (1988) *The Embryology of Behavior*, Mac Keith Press, Oxford

Goddard, S. A. (2002) *Reflexes, Learning and Behavior*, Fern Ridge Press, Eugene, Oreg.

Goodenough, F. L. (1926) *Measurement of Intelligence by Children's Drawings*, Harcourt Brace & World, New York

Grant, E. (1994) *Sexual Chemistry*, Mandarin Paperbacks, London

Halleck, R. P. (1898) *The Education of the Central Nervous System*, Macmillan Company, London

Hardy, A. (1956) *The Open Sea*, Collins, London

Harris, D. B. (1963) *Children's Drawings as Measures of Intellectual Maturity*, Harcourt Brace, New York

Johansen, K. V. (1992) *Sensory deprivation: A Possible Cause of Dyslexia*, Nordissk Tidsskrift for Spesialpedagogikk, Scandinavian University Press, Oslo

Johansen, K. V. (1994) Johansen Sound Therapy Training Course (sponsored by INPP), Chester

Kiphard, E. J. (2000) Personal communication

Lewis, C. S. (1956) *The Last Battle*, The Bodley Head, London

McMillan, M. (1930) *The Nursery School*, J. M. Dent, London

Madaule, P. (1993) *When Listening Comes Alive*, Moulin Publishing Company, Ontario

Madaule, P. (2001) The Ear Voice Connection Workshop. Seminar, Chester, November.

Milne, A. A. (1927) *Now We Are Six*, Methuen and Co. Ltd., London

Monroe, P. (1914) *A Textbook in the History of Education*, Macmillan Company, New York

Montessori, M. (1913), cited in Culverwell, E. P. (1913) *The Montessori Principle and Practice*, G. Bell & Sons Ltd.

Morgan, E. (1982) *The Aquatic Ape*, Souvenir Press Ltd., London

Morgan, E. (1990) *The Scars of Evolution*, Souvenir Press, London

Morgan, E. (1994) *The Descent of the Child*, Souvenir Press Ltd., London

Myers, J. J. and Sperry, R. W. (1985) 'Interhemispheric communication after section of the forebrain', *Cortex*, 21: 249-60

Naglieri, J. A. (1988) *DAP Draw a Person: A Quantitative Scoring System*, The Psychological Corporation, Harcourt Brace Jovanovich, Inc., New York

Nicolson, R., Fawcett, A., and Dean, P. (1994) 'Impaired performance of children with dyslexia on a range of cerebellar tests', *Annals of Dyslexia*, 46: 259-83

O'Dell, N. and Cook, P. (1996) *Stopping Hyperactivity: A New Solution*, Avery, New York

Odent, M. (1991) 'The early expression of the rooting reflex', Paper presented at the 4th European Conference of Neuro-Developmental Delay in Children with Specific Learning Difficulties, Chester

Odent, M. (1999) *The Scientification of Love*, Free Association Books, London

Odent, M. (2002) 'Bonding at birth', Paper presented at the Conference of the Society for Effective Affective Learning (SEAL), University of Derby, July 2002.

Palmer, L. (2003) Personal Communication

Panksepp, J. (1998) *Affective Neuroscience*, Oxford University Press, Oxford

Peiper, A. (1963) *Cerebral Function in Infancy and Early Childhood*, The International Behavioral Sciences, New York

Rauscher, F. and Shaw, G. (1996), *cited in Newsweek*, 19/2/96; 'Research findings show music can enhance key component of human intelligence', Summary of paper presented at the 102nd Annual Conference of the American Psychological Association

Riopelle, A. J. and Hubbard, D. C. (1977) 'Prenatal manganese deprivation and early behaviour of primates', *Journal of Ortho-Molecular Psychiatry*, 6: 327-33

Schilder, P. (1933) 'The vestibular apparatus in neuroses and psychoses', *Journal of Nervous and Mental Disease*, 78: 1–23, 137-64

Schore, A. N. (1994) *Affect Regulation and the Origin of the Self*, Laurence Erlbaum Associates, Hove, UK

Shakespeare, W. (16th century), *As You Like It*, Ch. 24

Tallal, P. (1996), reported in *The Register* (Eugene, Oreg.), 5th January

Tomatis, A. A. (1991) *The Conscious Ear*, Station Hill Press, Inc., Tarrytown, New York

Tomatis, A. A. (1991) *About the Tomatis Method*, The Listening Centre, Toronto, Ontario

Resources

The Institute for Neuro-Physiological Psychology was established by Psychologist, Dr Peter Blythe in 1975 to research into the effects of Central Nervous System dysfunction on learning and emotional behaviour and to devise protocols for assessment and effective treatment using physical programmes of remediation.

In addition to treating many children since 1975, INPP is also the training centre for professionals working in special needs and allied fields, from all over the world, who wish to use INPP's methods. Centres practising INPP's techniques exist in Sweden, Germany, Ireland, Spain, Italy, the Netherlands, the U.S.A., South America, Australia and the Far East.

Peter Blythe and Sally Goddard Blythe are the authors of a number of books including: *Stress, Drugless Medicine, An Organic Basis for Neuroses and Education Difficulties, A Teacher's Window into the Child's Mind and Reflexes, Learning and Behaviour.*

Details of all INPP contacts can be obtained from:

The Institute for Neuro-Physiological Psychology International
(INPP Ltd)
1, Stanley Street
Chester CH1 2LR
Tel/Fax (0)1244 311414
Email: mail@inpp.org.uk
Website: www. inpp.org.uk

INPP Scotland, Director, Sheila Dobie
2, Stoneycroft Road
Edinburgh EH30 9HX
Tel/Fax (0)131 331 4744
Email: inpp@ic24.net

Other Useful Addresses

Movement, Music and Early Learning
Jabadao Centre for Movement Studies
Branch House
Branch Road, Armley
Leeds S12 3AQ
0113 231 0650
Email: info@jabadao.org.uk

Choristers Schools Association
www.choirschools.org.uk

Dalcroze Society Inc.
100 Elborough Street
London SW18 5DL
Email: admin@dalcroze org.uk

Music and Dance Scheme
www.dfes.uk/mds

Sound Therapy Centres
Dyslexia Research Laboratory
Dr Kjeld Johansen
Rö Skolovej 14DK 3760
Gudhjem. Bornholm. Denmark
Email: kvj@dyslexic-lab.dk

The Tomatis Centre UK Ltd
3, Wallands Crescent
Lewes. East Sussex BN7 2QT

The Listening Centre
Paul Madaule
599 Markham Street
Toronto. Canada M6G 27L
Email: listen@idirect.com

Auditory Integrative Training
The Georgiana Foundation
PO Box 2607
Westport CT 06880
U.S.A.

The Listening Programme
Alex Doman
Advanced Brain Technologies
PO Box 1088
Ogden. Utah 84402. U.S.A.

SAMONAS
Dr. Ingo Steinbach
Klangstudio LAMBDOMA
Markgrafenufer 959071 Hamm. Germany

Dyslexia – Teaching and Research

British Dyslexia Association (BDA)
98, London Road
Reading RG1 5AV
Helpline 0118 9668271
Email: infor@dyslexiahelp-bda.demon.co.uk

Dyslexia Institute (DI)
Park House
Wick Road
Egham Surrey
01784 222300

Dr Harold Levinson
www.dyslexia-add.co.uk

Dyspraxia
The Dyspraxia Foundation
www.dyspraxiafoundation.org.uk

Attention Deficit and Hyperactivity
Hyperactive Children's Support Group HACSG
71, Whyke Lane
Chichester
West Sussex PO19 7PD
01243 551313
www.hacsg.org.uk

Pre-conceptual and Nutritional Information
Foresight
Association for the Promotion of Pre-conceptual Care
www.foresight-preconption.org.uk

Restorative Health Company
www.rehealth.com

Education and Early Learning
Montessori Teaching
www.montessori.edu

Steiner Waldorf Schools Fellowship
Kidbrooke Park
Forest Row
East Sussex. RH18 5JB
www.steinerwaldorf.org.uk

Appendix

Towards a Holistic Refoundation for Early Childhood: The Hawthorn Press 'Early Years Series'

> 'The early years of life provide a foundation for all later learning... If teaching is aimed at the child's developmental level, then effective learning will result.'
>
> Sally Goddard Blythe, *The Well Balanced Child*

Introduction: The Dismembering of Childhood

Founded several years ago with its first title, Russell Evans's *Helping Children to Overcome Fear*, the books in Hawthorn Press's pioneering 'Early Years' series – to which the present book is the latest addition – are providing parents and early-years workers with welcome and much-needed nourishment and inspiration in the face of modern culture's 'managerial' ethos of over-active, prematurely intellectual intrusion into *the very being* of young children. Since the mid-1990s, a formal-schooling ideology has been encroaching ever more insidiously into England's early years practice and policy-making – with the relentless bureaucratization of early learning environments stemming from, for example, mechanistic developmental assessments, centrally dictated 'Early Learning Goals', and the extraordinary imposition of a 'curriculum' on to children as young as 3. (I exclude Wales and Scotland from the worst features of these unfortunate tendencies, as their autonomy, based on a degree of political independence, has enabled them to pursue a significantly more progressive early childhood policy than the worst excesses of the technocratic English system. However, many of these trends are widely observable in the Western world.)

Here in Britain, for example, we read in the Times Educational Supplement of 17th January 2003 that reception teachers are now having to work their way through no less than 3,510 boxes to tick, as they are forced to assess every child against a staggering 117 criteria. This is in part, perhaps, symptomatic of the take-over of responsibility for early-childhood settings by OFSTED (the Office for Standards in Education), with the OFSTED inspectorate's 'surveillance culture' ideology cascading down the education system to the earliest of ages. Not without reason did the prominent sociologist, Professor Nikolas Rose, write some years ago that 'Childhood is the most intensively governed sector of personal existence'. A whole range of factors is continually reinforcing the cognitive 'hot-housing' atmosphere that pervades the education system – and which a number of eminent educationalists believe could well be doing untold harm to a generation of children. Yet a whole range of literature and research (see bibliography) is increasingly challenging the sanity of these trends; and the Hawthorn Press Early Years series is just one cultural manifestation of a deep and widespread disquiet with the manic politicization of early-years learning which has occurred with breathtaking rapidity – and with virtually no informed public or political debate – since the mid-late 1990s.

These trends represent a peculiar kind of 'madness' – symptoms of a manic 'modernity' whose one-sidedly materialistic values and practices are laying waste to much of what we all instinctively or intuitively know to be necessary for living a wholesome, nourishing life. While there seems to be an endless stream of narrowly conceived 'positivistic' research on our utilitarian education system's narrow obsession with 'driving up' standards and educational 'targets', there is little if any empirical research being carried out on the medium – and long-term effects on children's overall social and emotional development of the soullessly mechanistic educational 'regimes' to which they are unremittingly being subjected. This is nothing short of a national scandal, at which future, more enlightened generations will surely look back aghast at our crass immaturity and almost wilful neglect of what really matters in living a healthy life. Yet for anyone with a modicum of common sense, the symptoms of a profound malaise are there for all to see. Here, for example, are just a few headlines from a selection of articles in one popular national British newspaper over the period September to December 2002:

- 'Obese children "facing epidemic of diabetes"';
- '345,000 children are hit by behavioural disorder;
- 'More youngsters than ever own up to using drugs';
- 'Childhood drinking doubles in a decade';
- 'Rush to give morning-after pills to girls as young as 11';
- 'Shock as twice as many pupils under 16 found to be smokers';
- 'Me, me generation – stressed and self-centred, the young strive to succeed'.

Yet in the face of this mounting malaise, the mechanistic, 'modernizing' juggernaut simply ploughs on, apparently quite impervious to the insight that *its own policies and practices* are substantially contributing to this malaise, and are storing up a cultural disaster whose dimensions, together with its associated knock-on effects throughout society, can scarcely be dreamt of.

One common effect of these disturbing trends – and this is a recurrent theme throughout the series, not least in Sally Goddard Blythe's new book – is what we might call *the dismembering of childhood*. It would be all too easy to despair and give up in the face of these relentless modern trends; but as the books in the Early Years series compellingly demonstrate, there are tried and tested, viable alternatives to the aforementioned developments, grounded in a potent combination of perennial wisdom and cutting-edge research about child development, care, and learning. For, as Sally Goddard Blythe writes in her Introduction, 'intuition is the spark that lights the fire of scientific investigation. In looking at child development, I wanted to marry the processes of science and intuition...' – an intention which beautifully sums up a central aim of this book series. Certainly, there is a growing 'counter-cultural' public mood which is clamouring for a humane and demonstrably effective alternative to the deeply unsatisfactory fare currently on offer in 'mainstream society'.

The books in this series, not least *The Well Balanced Child*, have an overriding focus which is **holistic, informed**, and **practical** – offering readers state-of-the-art information for those who are involved in early-childhood settings (i.e. from birth to about 6 years), be they familial or professional. The books offer practical, theoretically informed insights into a whole range of early-years-related questions and issues – thereby making a major contribution to the global cultural movement of concerned parents that educationalist Neil Postman was referring to when he wrote: 'There are parents... who are defying the directives of their culture. Such parents are not only helping their children to have a childhood... Those parents... will help to keep alive a human tradition. [Our culture] is halfway toward forgetting that children need childhood. *Those who insist on remembering shall perform a noble service*'. Indeed, Postman's inspiring championing of childhood could hardly provide a more fitting epigram for the Hawthorn Press Early Years series.

Some Symptoms of Childhood's Dismemberment

Parents and early-years professionals alike are voicing ever-more-vocal disquiet about prevailing educational challenges to childhood and its systematic cultural dismemberment. Of course it is important not to impugn the motives of other approaches (e.g. to imply that they are somehow *deliberately* setting out to harm children) – for that would be patently absurd. Rather, this is a cultural, or *Zeitgeist* question rather than an exclusively personal one – and current mainstream approaches can certainly be challenged at this 'world-view' level, as the following discussion will illustrate.

In today's 'hyper-modernized' world, the damaging pressures on young children are relentless and ever-increasing. On BBC Radio 4's *Today* programme, for example, Anne Atkins recently described her routine experience of children *as young as three* being tested for entry into pre-schools; and in a *Times Educational Supplement* report, we read that

> 'Parents' fears... are fuelling a huge rise in private tuition, *particularly for primary-aged and pre-school children*... Parents spend around £100 million a year on personal tutors. *Some of this is spent on two-year-olds.* 'We have had a lot more enquiries about tuition for pupils preparing for key stage 1 and 2 national tests', said a spokeswoman for the Personal Tutors Agency... One child aged two-and-a-half received help from a Stepping Stones tutor. *The toddler had to point to his name on the blackboard and hone social skills to win a private nursery school place.*'

'Top Tutors, a London-based agency... said it had frequent requests from parents of two-year-olds for help, although it refused to take children under three...' (emphases added)

Little wonder, then, that the distorting effects of *anxiety* on healthy development and learning constitute a theme which recurs throughout the series. As Sally Goddard Blythe so presciently points out, 'Under conditions of... anxiety, play activity is markedly reduced or absent'. The crucial role of free creative play is repeatedly emphasized by a number of other series authors (Evans, Jenkinson, Oldfield, Rawson and Rose, Large): for as Professor Tina Bruce said to the Anna Freud Centenary Conference in November 1995, 'Play cannot be pinned down and turned into a product of measurable learning. This is because play is a process [which] enables a holistic kind of learning, rather than fragmented learning'.

Relatedly, and as the great educational and paediatric pioneers Susan Isaacs and Donald Winnicott compellingly demonstrated, the young child needs an *unintruded-upon space* in which to play with, elaborate, and work through her deepest wishes, anxieties, and unconscious fantasies. In turn, the child will thereby gain competence in healthily managing – with her own freely developed will – her curiosities and anxieties about human relationship. Sally Jenkinson's seminal Early Years book, *The Genius of Play*, develops these arguments at much greater length than I am able to here.

Another consistent theme in the Early Years series is the pernicious deforming effects on young children of *premature cognitive-intellectual development* – a theme which Sally Goddard Blythe addresses with great impact and effect in *The Well Balanced Child*. Here, we find convincing *neurological* as well as social rationales which argue against the one-sidedness of over-intellectually 'left-brain', *unbalanced* learning, particularly at young ages. As Professor Patrick Bateson and Paul Martin have written, 'Children who are pushed too hard academically, and who consequently advance temporarily beyond their peers, may ultimately pay a price in terms of lost opportunities for development'. Certainly, at least some Western governments are narrowly preoccupied with a control-obsessed mentality – leading to a child 'hot-housing' ideology which may well be harming a whole generation of children, as even the British Parliament's Education Select Committee has cautioned. Certainly, the

inappropriate and highly damaging pressures on young children do seem to be relentless and ever-increasing – at cultural as well as at purely educational levels.

We are already witnessing signs of the harm being done by a one-sidedly materialistic culture in general, and by the current early years educational regime in particular. A study by the National Health Foundation reports record levels of stress-related mental health problems in children. And one press report writes of the frightening scale of medically diagnosed child 'behavioural disorders', with 'tens of thousands of schoolchildren with mild behaviour problems [now] being drugged with Ritalin... simply in order to control them'. It is by no means far-fetched to propose some kind of causal relationship between the burgeoning and comparatively recent epidemic in child 'behavioural disturbances', and recent early years policy 'innovations' which demand a relentless and intrusive surveillance, measurement, assessment, and testing of children's developmental process – not to mention the forced imposition of adult-centric cognitive-intellectual learning at ever-earlier ages. I believe that the central arguments in *The Well Balanced Child* are certainly consistent with such a contention.

On this view, then, symptoms of so-called 'attention deficit disorder' and the like are surely far better understood as children's understandable response to, and unwitting commentary on, technological culture's ever-escalating manic overstimulation (cf. see Martin Large's book, *Set Free Childhood*) – and not least, its cognitively-biased distortions of early child development. Until our policy-makers develop the insight (and humility) to recognize and then respond to this malaise at a cultural and political level rather than at an individualized medical level, the prevalence of children's 'behavioural difficulties' will inevitably continue to escalate – Ritalin or no Ritalin.

Finally, and in harmony with the arguments in Sally Goddard Blythe's book, the Nobel Prize-winning physicist Murray Gell-Mannis is quite specific about the harm caused by *unbalanced* educational experience:

> an elementary school program narrowly restricted to reading, writing, and arithmetic will educate mainly one hemisphere [of the brain], leaving half of an individual's high-level potential unschooled. Has our society tended to overemphasize the values of an analytical

attitude, or even of logical reasoning? Perhaps in our educational system we lay too little emphasis on natural history.

Moreover, the very latest scientific brain research by F. Ostrosky-Solis and colleagues at the National Autonomous University in Mexico is corroborating these concerns, with their recent finding that learning to read and write does indeed demand interhemispheric specialization, with preliterate subjects showing patterns of brain activation that are significantly different from those of literate subjects. A clear implication of these findings is that *the forced, 'adult-centric' imposition of early literacy (and numeracy) learning on to the developing brains of young children is something that should only be pursued with extreme caution*: indeed, that at the very least, a strict 'precautionary principle' should be followed in this field, such that the onus of proof is on those who would press early formal learning to demonstrate that it is not harmful to the neurological development of young children, rather than the burden of proof lying with those who argue against the 'too much too soon' educational ideology. In short, there might, at last, be sound scientific-experimental evidence beginning to emerge for the view, long held in Steiner Waldorf circles, that *premature intellectual (left-brain) development is acutely harmful to young children's development.*

Re-membering Childhood: The Early Years Series

The principal focus of the Early Years series, then, is the promotion of healthy child development in its physical, emotional, and spiritual dimensions. Each book arises from parents' own pressing questions and concerns about their children, such as: 'Why is creative play important?'; 'How can I tell when my child is ready to start formal schooling?'; 'How can I help sick children?'; 'How can I learn to be a family story-teller?'; 'What is distinctive about Steiner (Waldorf) early childhood education?'; 'How can I most effectively nourish my young child's experience of music in the early years?'; 'What effective "holistic", balanced approaches are available for special needs children?' – and so on. The series is therefore very much driven by the experience of *parents themselves*, rather than being primarily professionally or 'expert'-driven, as is much of the early-years literature.

The distinctive approach represented in these books is strongly, but not exclusively, informed by the flourishing world-wide network of some 1,500 Steiner (Waldorf) Kindergartens, with the 80 years of accumulated wisdom on child development that this global movement has built up – founded on the original indications of the educationalist and philosopher Rudolf Steiner. The series freely draws upon the wisdom and insight of other prominent holistic approaches, including Froebel, Montessori (both featuring in *The Well Balanced Child*), and other respected holistic early-years specialists – thus embracing the emerging 'company of like-minded friends' (to adapt a phrase coined by Sally Jenkinson), working together in their distinct yet complementary ways for healthy child development.

A defining feature of each book is its focus on a specific topic or question for which parents, teachers, or other early years workers commonly require sound information and effective practical input. Books are based on up-to-date research and practice, and are written by an authority in the field in question. Hawthorn Press is working in close consultation with a range of parent educational organizations in developing the series – for example, Parent Network and Winston's Wish, the Steiner (Waldorf) Kindergarten movement, and the British Steiner Schools Fellowship, the Alliance for Childhood, and Human Scale Education. In this way, the issues that the series is covering are emerging organically from the concerns of parents and educators themselves in today's demanding and complex world.

Each book contains 'Resources' and Further Reading sections so that interested readers can follow up their interest in the field in question. Future books are envisaged on such prescient issues as: child development from a holistic perspective; music in the early years; Special Needs questions; holistic baby care; and creativity and the imagination in early childhood – to name just a few. Titles published to date are already proving to be ideal study-texts for reading, study, and support groups, as well as authoritative sources for holistic perspectives on early-years training courses of all kinds. Many books in the Early Years series promise to become *the* definitive works in their particular fields for many years to come, and have already received very favourable reviews and widespread acclaim from a range of sources right across the globe.

From *Helping Children Overcome Fear…*

This latter, the first book in the Early Years series, by Russell and Jean Evans, emphasizes the crucial importance of expression through free play; and explicitly recognizes the importance of the emotional and spiritual dimensions in early life. A consideration of fear and grief in early childhood is a particularly apt focus for the first book in the series, and for a number of reasons. First, the book highlights the way in which it is crucial that parents and professionals are aware of the *developmentally appropriate* needs of the child – and to relate with the child accordingly. As Professor David Elkind among many others has pointed out, children are not 'mini-adults', and are positively harmed through having to cope with *age-inappropriate demands.* This was also one of the many crucial developmental insights that Rudolf Steiner emphasized, and on which his original pedagogical indications for Steiner (Waldorf) education are based – and it also recurs throughout *The Well Balanced Child.*

Second, as is demonstrated by both psychoanalytic theory and the important work of Daniel Goleman in his celebrated book *Emotional Intelligence,* the feeling life plays a crucial yet often neglected role in the young child's world. As a leading academic in this field, Dr Judy Dunn, has put it,

'Emotions are at the center of children's relationships, well-being, sense of self, and moral sensitivity and are centrally linked to their increasing understanding of the world in which they grow up. Yet we have only recently begun to pay serious attention to the significance of children's emotions.'

Fear and anxiety are certainly 'core' emotions which all children must learn to cope with and healthily manage in a balanced and socially enabling way; and Jean Evans' book provides us with an exemplary holistic approach to the child's emotional world in what can often be an exceptionally demanding and alien environment – that of professional medical care.

Third, grief and loss are central to human experience; and the way in which young children are helped to integrate these primary human experiences can set up life-long 'templates' which in turn significantly influence both children's and adults' capacity for 'emotionally competent' and relatively non-neurotic relating in later life. Jean Evans' work again provides us with a wealth of insight into how these challenging emotions can be successfully worked with and integrated.

...via *The Genius of Play; Storytelling with Children; Free to Learn; Ready to Learn; Set Free Childhood; Kindergarten Education...*

Play and 'story' have traditionally been recognized as absolutely central accompaniments of a healthy, well-rounded education – and the Early Years books by Sally Jenkinson (*The Genius of Play*) and Nancy Mellon (*Storytelling with Children*) offer wonderfully inspiring testimonies to the importance of play and story in healthy child development. Recent research suggests that children who are deprived of stories in early life are statistically far more likely to grow up to possess anti-social criminological tendencies; and there is compelling reason to think that a similar fate might well await children who are deprived of creative, unintruded-upon play in early childhood (the celebrated High-Scope project in the USA certainly presents some suggestive corroborative evidence on this). Parents and educators wanting a comprehensive and heartening rationale for the importance of play and story could certainly do no better than to read, respectively, *The Genius of Play* and *Storytelling with Children*.

Steiner (Waldorf) education is one educational pedagogy which embodies both play and story in a comprehensive holistic framework which is developmentally attuned to the growing child in an explicit and fully theorized way. Lynne Oldfield's book *Free to Learn* represents the most comprehensive outline of Steiner (Waldorf) early-childhood education currently available in the English language, and in the comparatively short time since its publication it has already become *the* seminal text in this field – indispensable reading for all those seeking a sensitive and *sensible* alternative to the assessment-driven hot-housing mentality which currently saturates mainstream early-years learning environments.

The most up-to-date research on learning and the brain is beginning to confirm the insights bequeathed to us by Rudolf Steiner, and upon which Martyn Rawson and Michael Rose substantially draw in their Early Years book *Ready to Learn* (again, Goddard Blythe's book is essential reading in this regard). To take just one example, Steiner's indication to teach 'from the whole to the part' (rather than 'atomistically' from the part to the whole) is amply confirmed by neuro-psychologist Robert Ornstein when he recently wrote that, in education, 'We should emphasize more of a top-down approach – …first teaching the overall framework… We don't need a special right-brain learning program, but simply to put the large picture first in front of the student'. Rawson and Rose draw upon insights such as these to develop a systematic description of the main developmental processes involved in early learning and development, which in turn lay the essential foundation for later, more formal learning – or *school readiness*.

As do most of the books in this series, these authors draw heavily on Steiner's educational insights, implicitly adopting a *Goethean approach* which favours knowledge gained through personal experience, insight, and accumulated wisdom about child development, rather than through so-called 'objective' research and positivistically derived data (cf. Henri Bortoft's book *The Wholeness of Nature: Goethe's Way of Science*, Floris, 1996). It is in this context that holistically inclined, *genuinely balanced* learning, along the lines outlined in Oldfield's *Free to Learn*, Rawson and Rose's *Ready to Learn*, and Goddard Blythe's *The Well Balanced Child*, clearly becomes an absolute necessity for the future well-being of our modern world.

> Recent press stories are at last beginning to report accumulating research which is confirming the grave concerns about the harmful effects of televisual culture that the Steiner movement has been warning us about for decades. To take just one example, in *The Times* of the 2nd February 2004, we read a report headlined 'TV "hampering children's speech development"':
>
> 'Television viewing is affecting the verbal and communications skills of a growing number of pre-school age children, with some confused by simple questions such as "what would you like to play with?", a charity [I CAN] says.'

I CAN's survey of nursery staff found one in five workers saying that children often had difficulty explaining what they were doing, and almost *90 per cent* of nursery workers said that they thought the occurrence of speech, language, and communication difficulties was a growing problem amongst pre-school children, with one in three believing the problem to be growing significantly. The rise in the problem was attributed to a number of factors: the passive use of television was cited as a factor by 82 per cent of respondents; and additional comments predominantly criticised the use of videos and computers.

In 2003, the British Chief Inspector of Schools, David Bell, also said that the verbal and behavioural skills of five-year-olds appeared to be suffering; and the British Education Minister, Charles Clarke, has recently (January 2004) spoken out on the mal-effects of an unremitting diet of TV violence on the anti-social behaviour of young people. There are signs, indeed, that, notwithstanding the manifold vested interests mitigating against it, the message about the harm done by televisual culture is beginning to reach the highest political offices. In this context, Martin Large's well-received book *Set Free Childhood* explains in great detail the causal mechanisms involved, in the process performing a great service to those seeking a solid, convincing rationale for reducing or even eliminating the influence of the toxic 'screen culture' from their children's young lives.

Large's argument against the screen culture is especially germane to the concerns outlined earlier in this article – not least the burgeoning incidence of behavioural and 'deficit disorders' in young children. Yet what also becomes clear in Large's book is that we should not underestimate the vested material(istic) interests which wish to maintain and extend the status quo: for what we needs must address in all this – and urgently – is *political, institutional, and centralized economic power*. Moreover, as Large makes clear, Information Technology constitutes another highly contested terrain within early-years learning. The British Government's latest early-childhood policy guidance, *Curriculum Guidance for the Foundation Stage*, approvingly advocates – *and makes compulsory* – computer use and a strong ITC presence in all state-funded early years settings. Yet the findings of recent British Department for Education-funded research on the alleged educational benefits of (for example) computer games have been strongly challenged by Dr Aric Sigman, among others – challenges which are taken much further in Large's new book. Such narrowly circumscribed research, preoccupied as it is with cognitive-intellectual capacities at the expense of wholesome, rounded development, is indeed quite incapable of the kind of holistic, well-balanced perspective that is absolutely essential in a field concerned with the effects upon the vulnerable child's mind-brain of these relentless technological intrusions. We can only hope that the policy-makers might ultimately fund some telling psycho-sociological research on the possible link between this arid techno-world and the ever-mounting existential malaise, mental ill-health, and criminality manifesting in the lives of young people in Western culture.

Certainly, we should be deeply concerned when we find relatively conventional neuroscientists like Professor Susan Greenfield of Oxford University beginning to suggest that an increasingly ubiquitous Information Technology may entail profound long-term risks, including, as she writes, 'the potential loss of imagination, the inability to maintain a long attention span, the tendency to confuse fact with knowledge, and a homogenisation of an entire generation of minds'. 'These risks', she continues, 'could even actually change the physical workings of the brain'. For anyone even remotely concerned about these possible effects, Large's new book is indispensable reading.

At its best, the Kindergarten educational experience serves as at least some kind of antidote to the pernicious forces highlighted in this appendix; and in her recent book *Kindergarten Education*, the inspirational Californian Kindergarten teacher Betty Peck has given us an invaluable insight into her unique Kindergarten, distilling decades of experience of her work with young children. Many in the broad 'holistic' education movement passionately believe that *inspiration* is one of the most important qualities that teachers can bring to their relationships with children; and there is certainly no substitute for the kind of rich life experience and perennial wisdom which permeate Peck's wonderful book.

In *Kindergarten Education* you will find, in abundance, heart, soul, love, tenderness, wisdom, creativity and imagination, aliveness, wholeness, reverence, and wonder. What we find in these pages is a passionate refoundation of what I call *the art of being* with young children, in a way that intuitively understands the subtleties of a child's learning, and the importance of adults' *sensitively attuned* enabling role in it; that respectfully nourishes their unfolding individual developmental paths; and which above all acknowledges and nurtures reverence, wonder, co-operation, and social and emotional intelligence.

In entering Betty Peck's Kindergarten we find a refreshing alternative to the instrumental learning which has recently swamped early-childhood education in the developed world. *Kindergarten Education* beautifully describes just what it is possible to create in the Kindergarten, and we should be deeply grateful to Betty Peck for championing what is rapidly becoming a dying art by creating a book which communicates the very 'soul' of Kindergarten teaching in the midst of this bleak utilitarian age. As Betty Peck herself so aptly writes, 'The teacher is responsible for keeping alive the magic [of learning], in whatever form she can manage'.

...to *The Well Balanced Child*

> 'Learning is not just about reading, writing, and maths.... Learning begins in space... The years of optimum right-hemisphere development are years when learning is still strongly linked to sensory-motor activity.'
>
> Sally Goddard Blythe

The reader who has reached this far in this editorial appendix will no doubt already have read Sally Goddard Blythe's excellent book, so I shall not dwell on it at length here – except to say that this is a book that falls squarely and impressively in the tradition of Rudolf Steiner's educational philosophy. That is to say, it places equal emphasis and value upon both science and perennial wisdom, and it demonstrates a mature understanding of the holistic nature of learning, and the subtle interrelationships entailed in healthy early learning that by far transcends the crassly mechanistic approaches that dominate modern mainstream thinking and practice. As Goddard Blythe puts it:

> 'Whilst science – the testing of observations and ideas – constitutes an essential part of civilization and progress, intuition is the spark that lights the fire of scientific investigation. In looking at child development, I wanted to marry the processes of science and intuition, to find an explanation as to why certain social traditions and child-rearing practices have been consistently successful, despite a vastly changing world and a diversity of cultural ideals.'

The Well Balanced Child is a book that demonstrates all that is best in the emerging 'New Science' that will surely soon replace the tired and increasingly irrelevant world-view of 'modernity' and all its worst features – arid soullessness, technocratic 'control-freakery', over-intellectualization, and an abject inability to see the whole for the parts.

Conclusion: Finding a Better Way

These, then, are just some of the themes that recur in this leading-edge book series. There is a growing sense that the tide is now turning against those pernicious cultural forces that have been systematically dismembering childhood – and towards a re-membering of a holistic vision of childhood which recognizes the damage that is being wrought by modern culture, and which offers practical and effective alternatives. To take just a few examples: The highly welcome recent anthology *Education! Education! Education!* (edited by Stephen Prickett and Patricia Erskine-Hill) comprehensively takes apart 'the new positivism' that has engulfed modern mainstream educational environments. At the political level, both Wales and Northern Ireland have long since scrapped school League Performance Tables and, more recently, most of the SATS school-testing edifice; and Welsh Assembly Education Minister Jane Davidson has shown a refreshing open-mindedness in relaxing the over-academic pressures in Welsh early-years education. In 2003 Education Minister Charles Clarke surprised many by relaxing (albeit in a minor way) some of the worst excesses of the SATS testing regime for 7 year olds; and ministers may even be starting to consider the incontestable benefits deriving from a later start to formal schooling. To the extent that the Hawthorn Early Years series can buttress and reinforce this mounting sea-change in attitudes to childhood, it will have more than served its purpose.

  In sum, the key to building a better world surely lies in just how successfully we can facilitate our children's healthy development. Hawthorn Press's Early Years series is making available a rich range of books which will 'help parents defy the directives of modern culture' (Neil Postman), and *find a better way* to raise their children and help them realize their full potential. These books are helping parents and professionals alike to *reinvigorate* the rapidly disappearing art of *understanding children and their developmental needs*, which modern materialist culture has done so much to undermine; and both of these countervailing trends are comprehensively and illuminatingly illustrated in Sally Goddard Blythe's new book.

In this hyperactively modernized age, and as *The Well Balanced Child* clearly demonstrates, education has certainly become unhealthily skewed towards cognitively-orientated, so-called 'left-brain' learning, to the neglect of more holistic 'right-brain' learning, with the latter's specialization for 'the large strokes of a life's portrait' (to quote neuropsychologist Robert Ornstein), conveying emphases, subtext, and contextual meaning: in short, *overall context*. As Goddard Blythe writes in *The Well Balanced Child*, 'Although learning can take place at any stage in development, it is more efficient if it coincides with the time of neurological "readiness"'. One can hardly exaggerate just what is at stake in all this – for as Ornstein has written, 'We've built a world that often overwhelms our mind's native ability to manage. So our focus needs to shift from the smaller ones towards understanding the nature of the larger systems in which we live.'

Above all, the authors in the Early Years series would all surely agree that education should nourish and facilitate, rather than subvert, children's innate *love of learning* – as Ornstein has it: 'We're confronted with a large number of students and educators dissatisfied with the emphasis on drilling unrelated facts. Students [and children] lose interest, they don't see the relevance to their life... We're trained for drills and learning things without connecting them to the world.'

By way of closing, we invite you, the reader, to support this important series – and in so doing, to join the rapidly growing body of parents and educators who are determined to find a better way.

Richard House, Series Editor
Norwich, England
February 2004

Holistic Perspectives on Child Learning: Resource Bibliography

Note: Hawthorn Press 'Early Years' Series books are set in **bold** type.

ALLIANCE FOR CHILDHOOD (2000) *Fool's Gold: A Critical Look at Computers in Childhood*, College Park, Md

ANON (2000) 'Nursery lessons "damage" learning', *Times Educational Supplement*, 28th January, p. 6

BALDWIN DANCY, R. (2000) *You Are Your Child's First Teacher*, 2nd edn, Celestial Arts, Berkeley, Calif.

BROWN, T., FOOT, M., and HOLT, P. (2001) *Let Our Children Learn: Allowing Ownership, Providing Support, Celebrating Achievement*, Education Now Books, Nottingham (from 113 Arundel Drive, Bramcote Hills, Nottingham NG9 3FQ)

BROWNE, A. (2000) 'Mind-control drug threat for children', *The Observer* newspaper, 27th February, pp.1, 2

CARLTON, M. P. and WINSLER, A. (1998) 'Fostering intrinsic motivation in early childhood classrooms', *Early Childhood Education Journal*, 25 (3), pp. 159-65

CHARTER, D. (1998) 'Early learning may put boys off school', *The Times* newspaper, 24th March, p. 8

COLES, J. (2000) 'Hyper-parenting: are we pushing our children too hard?', *The Times* newspaper, 'Times 2' Supplement, 13th April, pp. 3-4

COYLE, D. (1999) 'What our children really need is a regime of benign neglect', *The Independent* newspaper (Review), 3rd August, p. 3

DeGRANDPRE, R. (2000) *Ritalin Nation: Rapid-Fire Culture and the Transformation of Human Consciousness*, W. W. Norton, New York

ELKIND, D. (1981) *The Hurried Child: Growing Up Too Fast Too Soon*, Addison-Wesley, Reading, Mass.

ELKIND, D. (1987) *Mis-education: Pre-schoolers at Risk*, A. A. Knopf, New York

ELKIND, D. (1990) 'Academic pressures – too much, too soon: the demise of play', in E. Klugman and S. Smilansky (eds), *Children's Play and Learning: Perspectives and Policy Implications*, Teachers College Press, Columbia University, New York, 1990, pp. 3-17

EVANS, R. (2000) *Helping Children to Overcome Fear: The Healing Power of Play*, Hawthorn Press, Stroud

FARENGA, P. (2000) 'The importance of computers in education does not compute', in R. Miller (ed.), *Creating Learning Communities*, Foundation for Educational Renewal/Solomon Press, Brandon, VT, pp. 192-4

FISHER, A. L. (2000) 'Computer caution', in R. Miller (ed.), *Creating Learning Communities*, Foundation for Educational Renewal/Solomon Press, Brandon, VT, pp. 195-8

FISHER, R. (2000) 'Developmentally appropriate practice and a national literacy strategy, *British Journal of Educational Studies*, 48 (1), pp. 58-69

HALLER, I. (1991) *How Children Play*, Floris Books, Edinburgh

HALPIN, T. (2001a) 'Why four is just too young to start lessons at school', *Daily Mail*, 12th January, p. 45

HALPIN, T. (2001b) 'Children can start school at six, says new Minister', *Daily Mail*, 28th June, p. 17

HARRIS, S. (2001) 'Hyper-parents beware: hot-housing "is making children ill"', *Daily Mail* newspaper, 22nd February, p. 17

HARTLEY-BREWER, E. (2001) *Learning to Trust and Trusting to Learn*, Institute for Public Policy Research, London (www.ippr.org.uk)

HEALY, J. M. (1990) *Endangered Minds: Why Children Don't Think and What We Can Do about It*, Touchstone/Simon & Schuster, New York

HEALY, J. M. (1998) *Failure to Connect: How Computers Affect Our Children's Minds – for Better and Worse*, Simon & Schuster, New York

HOUSE, R. (2000) 'Psychology and early years learning: affirming the wisdom of Waldorf', *Steiner Education*, 34 (2), 10-16

HOUSE, R. (2001) 'Whatever happened to holism?: Curriculum Guidance for the Foundation Stage – a Critique', *Education Now: News and Review*, 33, p. 3

HOUSE, R. (2002a) 'Loving to learn: protecting a natural impulse in a technocratic world', *Paths of Learning*, 12 (Spring), pp. 32-6

HOUSE, R. (2002b) 'The central place of play in early learning and development', *The Mother*, 2 (Summer) 2002, pp. 44-6

HOUSE, R. (2002-3) 'Beyond the Medicalisation of "Challenging Behaviour"; or Protecting our children from "Pervasive Labelling Disorder"', *The Mother* magazine, issues 4-7 (in four parts)

HOUSE, R. (2003) 'Soul-subtlety in the Kindergarten: Robert Sardello's Twelve Virtues as a Path of Personal and Professional Development', *Kindling* magazine, no. 4 (Autumn), pp. 16-18

HOUSE, R. (forthcoming) *The Trouble with Education: Stress, Surveillance and Modernity*, The Mother Publications, Glassonby

INSTITUTE FOR PUBLIC POLICY RESEARCH (2001) 'Exam mania could scar children's emotional health', press release, 24th August (www.ippr.org.uk)

JAFFKE, F. (2000) *Work and Play in Early Childhood*, Floris Books, Edinburgh

JENKINSON, S. (2001) *The Genius of Play: Celebrating the Spirit of Childhood*, **Hawthorn Press, Stroud**

JUDD, J. (1998) 'Children's learning suffers if they start school too soon', *The Independent* newspaper, 25th January

KIRKMAN, S. (2001) 'Parents' fears trigger private tuition boom', *Times Educational Supplement*, 19th October, p. 1

LARGE, M. (1992) *Who's Bringing Them Up? How to Kick the TV Habit*, **2nd edition, Hawthorn Press, Stroud**

LARGE, M. (2003) *Set Free Childhood: Parents' Survival Guide to Coping with Computers and TV*, **Hawthorn Press, Stroud**

LAURANCE, J. (1999) '"Holistic" children can fight allergies', *The Independent* newspaper, 30th April

LEONARD, T. (2003) 'The 5-year-olds hooked on telly: it's turning our kids into dunces', *Daily Star* newspaper, 3rd September, p. 6

MACINTYRE, C. (2001) *Enhancing Learning through Play: A Developmental Perspective for Early Years Settings*, David Fulton, London

McVEIGH, T. and WALSH, N. P. (2000) 'Computers kill pupils' creativity', *The Observer* newspaper, 24th September, p. 14

MAUDE, P. (2001) *Physical Children, Active Teaching: Investigating Physical Literacy*, Open University Press, Buckingham

MEDVED, M. & MEDVED, D. (1998) *Saving Childhood: Protecting Our Children from the National Assault on Innocence*, HarperCollins, Zondervan

MELLON, N. (2000) *Storytelling with Children*, Hawthorn Press, Stroud

MILLS, D. and MILLS, C. (1997) 'Britain's Early Years Disaster: Part 1 – The Findings', mimeograph

MOORE, R. S. & MOORE, D. N. (1975) *Better Late than Early: A New Approach to Your Child's Education*, Reader's Digest Press (Dutton), New York

OLDFIELD, L. (2001a) *Free to Learn: Introducing Steiner Waldorf Early Childhood Education*, Hawthorn Press, Stroud

OLDFIELD, S. (2001b) 'A holistic approach to early years', *Early Years Educator*, 2 (12), pp. 24-6

ORNSTEIN, R. (1997) *The Right Mind: Making Sense of the Hemispheres*, Harcourt Brace, New York

OSTROSKY-SOLIS, F., GARCIA, M. A., AND PÉREZ, M. (2004) 'Can learning to read and write change the brain organization? An electrophysiological study', *International Journal of Psychology*, 39 (1), pp. 27-35

PATTERSON, B.J. and BRADLEY, P. (2000) *Beyond the Rainbow Bridge: Nurturing Our Children from Birth to Seven*, Michaelmas Press, Amesbury, Mass.

PECK, B. (2004) *Kindergarten Education – Freeing Children's Creative Potential*, Hawthorn Press, Stroud

POSTMAN, N. (1994) *The Disappearance of Childhood*, Vintage Books, New York

PRICKETT, S. (2002) 'Managerial ethics and the corruption of the future', in S. Prickett and P. Erskine-Hill (eds), *Education! Education! Education!: Managerial Ethics and the Law of Unintended Consequences*, Imprint Academic, Thorverton, Britain, pp. 181-204

PROFESSIONAL ASSOCIATION OF TEACHERS (2000) *Tested to*

Destruction? A Survey of Examination Stress in Teenagers, PAT, London

PYKE, N. (2003) 'Do tests fail children?', *The Independent* (Education suppl.), 6th November, pp. 4-5

RAWSON, M. and ROSE, M. (2002) *Ready to Learn: From Birth to School Readiness*, Hawthorn Press, Stroud

RIDDELL, M. (2002) 'This exams madness', *The Observer* newspaper, 9th June

SALTER, J. (1987) *The Incarnating Child*, Hawthorn Press, Stroud

SANDERS, B. (1995) *A is for Ox: The Collapse of Literacy and the Rise of Violence in an Electronic Age*, Vintage Books, New York

SCHWEINHART, L.J. and WEIKART, D. P. (1997) *Lasting Differences: The High/Scope Preschool Curriculum Comparison Study through Age 23*, High/Scope Press, Ypsilanti, MI; Monographs of the High/Scope Educational Research Foundation No. 12

SHARP, C. (1998) 'Age of starting school and the early years curriculum', paper presented at the National Foundation for Educational Research Annual Conference, London, October (available at www.nfer.ac.uk/conferences/early.htm)

SHLAIN, L. (1998) *The Alphabet and the Goddess: The Conflict between Word and Image*, Viking Penguin, New York

SMITHERS, R. (2000) 'Exams regime "harms pupils"', *The Guardian* newspaper, 4th August, p. 1

STEINER, R. (1995) *The Kingdom of Childhood*, Anthroposophic Press, Hudson, New York

STEINER EDUCATION (2000) Special Issue: 'Caring for Childhood: Waldorf and the Early Years Debate', Vol. 34, No. 2

THOMSON, J. B. & others (1994) *Natural Childhood: A Practical Guide to the First Seven Years*, Gaia Books, London

TWEED, J. (2000) 'Mental health problems rise in all children', *Nursery World*, 6th April, pp. 8-9

REFLEXES, LEARNING, & BEHAVIOR: A WINDOW INTO THE CHILD'S MIND
by Sally Goddard

This unique and brilliant book explores the physical basis of learning difficulties, dyslexia, dyspraxia, Attention Deficit Disorder (ADD) and Attention Deficit Hyperactivity Disorder (ADHD), with particular focus on the role of abnormal reflexes and the effect upon subsequent development.

Sally Goddard, Director of the Institute for Neuro-Physiological Psychology, Chester, explains how the reflexes of infancy (primitive and postural) can affect the learning ability of the child if they not inhibited and integrated by the developing brain in the first three years of life. Each reflex is described, together with its function in normal development, and its impact upon learning and behaviour if it remains active beyond the normal period.

Simple tests for the reflexes that are crucial to education are described, together with suggestions for suitable remedial intervention. A brief history of how current methods of intervention designed to correct abnormal reflexes have evolved is included, together with a summary of some of the relevant research in the field.

This book is essential reading for parents, teachers, psychologists, optometrists, and anyone involved in the assessment, education, and management of children and their problems. It explains why certain children are unable to benefit from the same teaching methods as their peers, and why they remain immature in other aspects of their lives.

Please enclose a cheque for £21 (sterling) made payable to INPP Ltd. and complete and return the form to the address below:

ORDER FORM (*REFLEXES, LEARNING, AND BEHAVIOR*)
INPP, 1, Stanley Street, Chester. CH1 2LR, UK.
Tel/Fax 01244 311414
NAME..ADDRESS.................
....
....
....
POSTCODE........................
Tel. No......................................
EMAIL...
No. of copies @ £21 each ☐   Cheque enclosed for ☐

Postage outside Europe £2.00 extra

Other Books from Hawthorn Press

Free to Learn

Introducing Steiner Waldorf early childhood education

LYNNE OLDFIELD

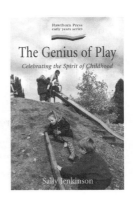

Free to Learn is a comprehensive introduction to Steiner Waldorf kindergartens for parents, educators and early years' students. Lynne Oldfield illustrates the theory and practice of kindergarten education with stories, helpful insights and lively observations.

'Children are allowed freedom to be active within acceptable boundaries; who are in touch with their senses and the environment; who are self-assured but not over-confident; who are developing their readiness to receive a formal education – in short, children who are free to be children and "free to learn".'

Kate Adams, *International Journal of Children's Spirituality*

256pp; 216 x 138mm; 1 903458 06 4; pb

The Genius of Play

Celebrating the spirit of childhood

SALLY JENKINSON

The Genius of Play addresses what play is, why it matters, and how modern life endangers children's play. Sally Jenkinson's amusing, vivid observations will delight parents and teachers wanting to explore the never-ending secrets of children's play.

'Enchanting photos and vignettes of young children at play ... do enjoy the account of the 'wedding dress den' and the old Suffolk recipes for 'preserving children.' Marian Whitehead, *Nursery World*

224pp; 216 x 138mm; 1 903458 04 8; pb

Ready to Learn

From birth to school readiness

MARTYN RAWSON AND MICHAEL ROSE

Ready to Learn will help you to decide when your child is ready to take the step from kindergarten to school proper. The key is an imaginative grasp of how children aged 0-6 years learn to play, speak, think and relate between birth and six years of age.

'Sound points about the risks of making developmentally inappropriate demands, including the headlong rush to get children to read and write ever earlier.'

Jennie Lindon, *Nursery World*

192pp; 216 x 138mm; 1 903458 15 3; pb

Set Free Childhood

Parents' survival guide to coping with computers and TV

MARTIN LARGE

Children watch TV and use computers for five hours daily on average. The result? Record levels of learning difficulties, obesity, eating disorders, sleep problems, language delay, aggressive behaviour, anxiety – and children on fast forward. However, *Set Free Childhood* shows you how to counter screen culture and create a calmer, more enjoyable family life.

'A comprehensive, practical and readable guide… the skilful interplay between academic research and anecdotal evidence engages the reader.'

Jane Morris-Brown, *Steiner Education*

240pp; 216 x 138mm; 1 903458 43 9; pb

Storytelling with Children

NANCY MELLON

Telling stories awakens wonder and creates special occasions with children, whether it is bedtime, around the fire or on rainy days. Nancy Mellon shows how you can become a confident storyteller.

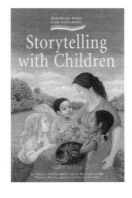

'Nancy Mellon continues to be an inspiration for storytellers old and new. Her experience, advice and suggestions work wonders. They are potent seeds that give you the creative confidence to find your own style of storytelling.'

Ashley Ramsden, Director of the School
of Storytelling, Emerson College

192pp; 216 x 138mm; illustrations; 1 903458 08 0 ; pb

Kindergarten Education

Freeing children's creative potential

BETTY PECK

Educator Betty Peck celebrates the power of Kindergarten to help children find their creativity and imagination – opening the door to a passionate relationship with learning. The result is an essential resource for teachers and parents who want to give their children a meaningful education.

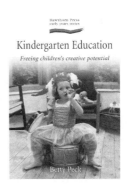

'This is an astonishing, impressive and magnificent work. ... this is must reading for every parent, would-be parent and teacher world-wide.'

Joseph Chilton Pearce, author 'Magical Child'

224pp; 216 x 138mm; 1 903458 33 1; pb

Getting in touch with Hawthorn Press

We would be delighted to receive your feedback on Kindergarten Education.

Visit our website for details of the Education and Early Years Series and books for parents, plus forthcoming books and events:

http://www.hawthornpress.com

Ordering books

If you have difficulties ordering Hawthorn Press books from a bookshop, you can order online at **www.hawthornpress.com** or you can order direct from:

United Kingdom
Booksource
32 Finlas Street, Glasgow
G22 5DU
Tel: (08702) 402182
Fax: (0141) 557 0189
E-mail: orders@booksource.net

USA/North America
Steiner Books
PO Box 960, Herndon
VA 20172-0960
Tel: (800) 856 8664
Fax: (703) 661 1501
E-mail: service@steinerbooks.org